XX

ALSO BY CAMPBELL McGRATH

XX

CAMPBELL
McGRATH

ecco

An Imprint of HarperCollins *Publishers*

HarperCollins books may be purchased for educational, business, or sales promotional use. For information please e-mail the Special Markets Department at SPsales@harpercollins.com.

FIRST EDITION

Designed by Mary Austin Speaker

Library of Congress Cataloging-in-Publication Data has been applied for.

ISBN 978-0-06-242735-9

16 17 18 19 20   OV/RRD   10 9 8 7 6 5 4 3 2

For the twentieth century

Acknowledgments

Poems from this collection have previously appeared in the following publications, whose editors I would like to thank: *5 a.m., American Poetry Review, Antioch Review, Berkeley Poetry Review, Black Renaissance Noire, Catalyst* (NZ), *Fogged Clarity, Green Mountains Review, Harvard Review, Hinchas de Poesia, Iowa Review, Jai-Alai Magazine, Kenyon Review, Michigan Quarterly Review, MiPOesias, New Ohio Review, Plume, Poem-a-Day* (Academy of American Poets), *Poetry Daily, Salmagundi, Terminus Magazine, White Review* (UK), *Yale Review*.

Several of these poems appeared in the chapbook *Picasso/Mao*, as part of the Floodgate Poetry Series, Upper Rubber Boot Books, 2014.

"The Style for Dylan (1965)" appeared in *How to Write About Music*, edited by Ally-Jane Grossan and Marc Woodworth, Bloomsbury Academic, 2015.

A letterpress edition of "Andy Warhol: Image, Print, Negative" appeared in the exhibition *Vanishing Points: Paint and Paintings from the Debra and Dennis Scholl Collection* at the Bass Museum of Art, 2011.

"Orson Welles: The Stage (1935)" was produced as a limited-edition broadside by Amanda Keeley, for the SWEAT II Broadside Collective, Miami, FL, 2014.

Of my century, in which, and not in any other, I was ordered to be born, to work, and to leave a trace.

—CZESŁAW MIŁOSZ

Century o century of clouds

—GUILLAUME APOLLINAIRE

Bound, hungry to pluck again from the thousand
technologies of ecstasy

boundlessness, the world that at a drop of water
rises without boundaries

I push the PLAY button:--

—FRANK BIDART, "FOR THE TWENTIETH CENTURY"

Contents

BOOK TWO

BOOK THREE

BOOK FOUR

BOOK FIVE

XX

Epilogue: 2016

Like prose does the term of our days extend
to the margin of the page
but it does not return, with a slap and a clang,
in the manner of an old typewriter carriage,
elementary mechanism
of spring-bearing levers and bird-claw glyphs.

Already I have journeyed more than a decade
into this pathless new millennium,
weary explorer who will never reach the pole.

Friends travel beside me, traipsing ahead,
falling by the wayside in the obdurate whiteness
from which all things of purpose have been carved away,
all things parsed and compassed by the wind.

Children follow in our tracks, assuming,
each time we look back, the aspect of strangers;
they exceed us as Olympian gods surpassed the Greeks
who fashioned them in their,
and thus our own, entirely mortal image.

And the illustrious, hard-frozen ocean receding
further into memory with each embattled step,
great whales feeding in the darkness,
their souls like wells of fragrant oil,
the exodus-light of icebergs made plastic
and manifest, that index, that sign.

To the margin but no more.

Like dough which rises to fill the baker's pan
with a scent of yeast and distant wheat fields,
leaving nothing in its aftermath
but a ruin of crusts, a scattering of crumbs,
avenues for the triumphal procession of the ants.

BOOK ONE

Picasso (1900)

Arrived in Paris with Casagemas to discover
Montmartre embodies a dream fulfilled,
a riot of cobblestones, stray dogs and peddlers,
baroque bird kiosks as in Barcelona, windmills
on the butte and all variety of street theater,

sculptors and anarchists and visionary drunks,
hurdy-gurdy music, melancholy *saltimbanques*,
dance-hall whores we cannot afford
and carefree models amidst oil cans and litter,
everything given license, everything on offer,
everything varnished with tinsel and glitter.

Already I abandon all concern with the past,
with Velázquez and Spanish *sombra*—
from this moment my painting is recast
in the galvanic mold of the modern era.
Now, at nineteen, I seize my destiny at last.

The die is cast, the Rubicon crossed,
and my only regret is to have lost
eighteen years of my life to a paternity
so parochial and antique. As blood rules the heart
thus electric current will fuel the twentieth century
and so I myself shall figure in its art.

Hearts of Darkness: Freud and Conrad (1901)

Messages from the interior: darkness & illumination,
dreams & blood. Two springs from whence arise
twin rivers coursing from the ego's murderous dream-empire.
What cargo they carry shall define the coming century:
ivory & guns, African blood congealed to profit,
Arbeit macht frei. Out of the heart of Congolese darkness

& into the mind's diamond mine, psychic darkness
evolving toward, if not light, then, enlightenment?
Century of chains & emancipations, empathy & greed.
Century of wraiths & indeterminacy, century of earth-rise,
o eager, anguished, totalitarian century!
Century of transistor gizmos, century of quantum dreams.

Freud's first lectures on *The Interpretation of Dreams*
drew a dozen listeners; proper Vienna would not darken
his door or its good name. Still the ghost of the century
rises from his grave like a genie from its lamp,
as from the burning furnace of the self dreams rise
to the lure of the imago, the masked dance of desire,

sexual dominance sublimated into boardroom money-lust.
What haunted Conrad's exiled London dreams
was not Belgian savagery but visions of elephants rising
to crash all night through the blind jungle darkness
within him, animals limned in bullion-light,
golden idols sacrificed to a market-driven century.

A century of propaganda & sales pitches, a century
of smoke & mirrors & incorporated gluttony.
The cathexis of Empire begets decolonialism's firestorm,

one last century held hostage to European dreams—
Rothschild & Marx, Freud & Einstein, Hitler's dark
parody of power & Picasso's *mirada fuerte*. What rises

must fall; what we repress consumes us, starfish at tide-rise.
A century of signs & design & *Dasein*, a century
of loss, like all the others. A century of children's small dark
hands severed by machetes as a lesson in productivity
from King Leopold. Kurtz & Conrad are dream-twins,
Id & Ego, Mengele & Freud, darkness & light.

O, century of atomic darkness,
rise
toward the dream-radiance for which you hunger.

Picasso (1902)

Yesterday walked across all of Paris in the snow
with a pastel rolled beneath my arm,
a pastiche of doting bourgeois mothers and children
with a vase of flowers, no less, utter and complete
artistic prostitution, only to find the dealer
is broke and cannot part with even ten francs.
I left it with her for nothing and trudged home
to the attic tenement I share with a verminous
and disreputable sculptor named Agero,
generous fellow to house a destitute countryman
but still a filthy disgrace. Like Van Gogh
I must survive on biscuits and water,
lacking even a candle to work by, making do
with chalk and ink on cheap paper,
scraps of canvas found or stolen on the sly.
I've done worse, pocketing change from Rocarol,
hiding stale bread crusts in my overcoat,
jotting pornographic sketches for the vile troop
of degraded Spaniards that roam the Hôtel du Maroc.
Pride forbids me to show my face to those
who envied my success eighteen months ago
and only Max Jacob offers comfort.
He considers my misfortune an epitome of genius
reduced to squalor, and I concur. So far
this third trip to Paris falls little short of disaster
and I lack even the price of a ticket home.
At least I shall survive the week, as Max promises
dinner at a café: omelettes and fried potatoes
may yet rekindle my affection for this frigid city
on which I, owning nothing, have staked everything.

Anna Akhmatova (1903)

Barely fifteen and already men are declaring
their love for her, grown men, and already she knows
she will drag their bodies across the white fire
of her nights as surely as she will sweep
the romance of the past behind her into this, her world.
She will bear the torch of the nineteenth century
into the present as Rilke carried a single iris
before his throat as he walked the streets of the city
to shield him from the monstrosity of mundane reality.

Ten years earlier, the first family photographs
are sepia prints: white gloves, a sailor's suit,
spring in the Crimea smelling of lilacs.
Ten years later, the first drawing is Modigliani's
erotic glyph, a sleek nude modernist arc,
the first paintings Cubist, Futurist, Acmeist.
Amid the studied decadence of the Stray Dog Café
she is a pale flower of the demimonde,
disdain for everything earthly and unexalted
scribbled in heroic stanzas across her face.
Ten more years and already she is famous
and already her voice is drowned
beneath the cadence of boots and rifles,
her verse denounced by Trotsky
as frivolously personal, archaically devout.
Another decade and she is reading Dante aloud
as Mandelstam weeps openly at the words—
mere words, mind you—days before the Party
swept him up in its grasp and he was gone.
She, who vowed to subsist on the sublime,
who could barely boil a potato or mend a sock,

living a life of denials and false confessions,
police officers knocking at the door,
the hasty burning of papers, again and again.
Why this portion for your children,
O Lord, terror and suffering and helplessness,
delivered from tyranny to tyranny,
day after day before the unblinking eye
of the prison gate, desperate for any word,
any sign of the vanished—why, O Lord?
Ten years to fame, twenty to famine,
thirty to the Terror, forty to the starving winter
of Leningrad under siege, fifty to the thaw,
sixty to an unanticipated old age
of vodka, ghosts and cabbage soup,
to the grey indeterminacy called,
in the corrupt modern idiom life, *real life.*

Barely fifteen, smelling of lilacs and April rain,
already the men swearing passionate vows
not one of them intends to keep.

Henry Ford (1904)

From curiosity comes dynamism, from obstinacy drive.

From the drawing board, from tinkering, from the machine shop in
the old barn come pistons and cams.

From gasoline comes internal combustion, comes a world of rubber
wheels instead of horseshoes, a world powered not by steam or
wind but oil refracted into a rainbow of mechanical possibility,
smoke and stink of it filling the little house on Bagley Avenue.

From the precision of clockmakers, from the gunworks of Samuel
Colt come interchangeable parts.

From the Arsenal of the Doge's Venice comes standardized
production.

From the butchery of hogs hung for slaughter, from Chicago packing
houses comes the conveyor belt, comes the assembly line, comes
the dismemberment of human toil.

From the builders of every monumental construct back to the Great
Pyramid of Cheops comes the mobilization of labor,

comes mass production,

comes the pace of the century and its mode of transport and its
consumerist destiny,

comes Highland Park, Hamtramck, River Rouge,

comes the river of ash and coke, river of bitumen, river of liquid
capital, river of molten vanadium steel,

comes the thunder of the blast furnace,

comes the glory of industry,

comes the abjection and abandonment of industry,

comes the world's first billionaire, the titan, the crank,

but not yet, all things in due course,

but not yet.

For now it is a cold afternoon in January,
and Henry Ford has just established a new world speed record
driving a first-of-its-kind Model B roadster at 91 mph
along a four-mile track on the soot-covered ice of Lake Saint Clair,
and afterwards he celebrates with a complimentary muskrat dinner
for himself and his entourage at the Chesterfield Hotel—
the Dodge Brothers are there, drinking heavily,
James Couzens, Harold Wills, the ace mechanic Spider Huff—

and for this moment he is not worried about magneto coils or engine
    blocks,
about investors or salesmen or the burgeoning competition,
about the Jews and their secret cabals or the goddamn unions
    ruining the country,

for now he sees only the sugar-fine granules of frozen dust
driven across the ice in snake-thin runnels,
their fluid aerodynamics

and the kinetic grace of the invisible force
that scours and propels them
in a model of ruthless simplicity—

Henry Ford is staring out the window,
lost in thought, stealing
everything he can from the wind.

Einstein's Clock (1905)

Something is ticking. Outside the window of the patent office
the famous fifteenth-century clock is marking the passage of hours,
of minutes and seconds, one after the other, as trains arrive
at the Bern station disgorging passengers into orderly streets,
one after the other, passengers with cases and parcels, one after the next,
the way light, in Einstein's understanding, moves in serial packets,
discrete quanta. The word *photon* is not in any dictionary;
the term *quantum mechanics* does not appear in the scientific record.
In Paris, the Curies are working to isolate pure radium,
for which Marie will receive her second Nobel Prize in 1911;
the luminous new metal will be prized for use on watch dials
and as a healthy additive to chocolate and drinking water.
Jean-Paul Sartre is born. Ayn Rand is born. Jules Verne dies.
Chekhov has been dead since July but Tolstoy has five years to live.
Joyce is teaching English in Trieste, Beckett will be born next year.
George Orwell is two: the sun will never set on the British Empire.
Picasso is playing billiards with Apollinaire in Montmartre
while the Wright Brothers have adopted an anhedral wing
to counteract pitch instability on *Wright Flyer III*.
Everything is motion, velocity, electrochemical transformation,
wave, particle, field. The Trans-Siberian Railway opens.
Las Vegas is founded on one hundred acres of desert auctioned off
by the San Pedro, Los Angeles & Salt Lake Railroad.
The century is gaining traction, the century is full of steam,
trains are running down the tracks of Einstein's imagination.
Suppose lightning struck the line at points A and B?
How could we determine simultaneity, relative to what constant?
There is a mirror on the train, a ray of candlelight, a rod,
the hands of a clock, a twin left behind on the platform.
Suppose he could run beside a beam of light at its own pace,
what would he see? Who constitutes an objective observer?

What is the fixed measure, where is the point of rest?
How can time be the divine absolute proposed by Newton
when it is a variable in the equation, when it is woven into the fabric,
we are swallows stitched into its sky, salamanders in its stream,
we are Escher's swallows transforming into salamanders,
century of phenomenological fragments, fractal & abstract,
century of schism & cataclysmic ventriloquism,
century of pleas & eurekas, apologias & diktats.
Bern's famous clock tower, the Zytglogge, has served
during its complicated history as a fortified guard post
and a prison for women accused of "intimacy" with priests.
Its lesser bell rings on the quarter hour and then,
upon the hour, a bearded figure of Chronos strikes
with his hammer the great bronze bell, cast in 1405.
The several massive clockfaces display not only the time
but days of the week, phases of the moon, houses of the zodiac;
the western face depicts Adam and Eve's eviction from Paradise,
the eastern a panoply of the planets represented as Roman gods
in accordance with Ptolemaic cosmography. In essence,
it illustrates every ethos, astronomical measure and belief system
from the Greeks through the Renaissance to the Enlightenment.
From the windowsill of his dusty office Einstein observes
the seconds count down toward noon, checking against his watch.
He has brought a lunch of sausage, rye bread, apples and tea,
and has stashed in his drawer some notes he is eager to complete
for a short, deductive paper on the relation of mass and energy.
He wishes, just this once, that time would move a little faster.

Matisse: Paris (1906)

Last year, the laughter of the crowds at sight of my paintings
could be heard from the doorway of the Salon des Indépendants,
but this year, while my new work erupts with joyful, unfettered color,
their derisive howls echo even beyond the streets of the quartier,
    across the rooftops of Paris and the beet fields of Flanders alike,
united only by their scorn for my art.

So be it. They wound me
but I begin to bleed less, I begin to believe
my pictures will sell and this time of tribulations pass.

To turn from the path of easy prosperity in the approved style has
    cost me everything,
even the hard-won credence of my father, whose agonized grimace
    betrays his opinion of *Le Bonheur de Vivre,*
dismissed by the critics as childish scribbling, as mere dye-work,
as if I had never outgrown my boyhood amongst the cottage-looms of
    Bohain.

There is nothing romantic in the poverty of artists except to those
    who ogle the starving,
as I recall them gasping at the absinthe-hollowed skull of Paul Verlaine
dressed like a destitute rake in the wineshops of the Rue Saint-Jacques,
figure of a fate to be avoided through iron discipline, relentless work,
    and luck.

What else can I call this wild visitation but fortune's grace?
Who guides my hand if not the muse herself?

Whether myself or another shall prove its agent, in the end I am
   certain
my new approach speaks to the true and essential art of the future.
The laughter of the mob will not drown out that voice.
Color will achieve its triumphal vindication.
As Derain said, this summer at Collioure, *the light throws up on all*
   sides its vast and clamorous shout of victory.

Picasso & Fernande Olivier (1907)

Fernande

Of course we are poor, but if Pablo sells a charcoal
he buys a roll of canvas, a sack of coal
for the stove, and a bottle of perfume to spoil me.
We eat bread and wine and pots of spaghetti,

sometimes we smoke opium,
which excites him,
or drink at Vernin's until all hours
with his rogue's gallery of cronies and connivers,
Catalan sculptors, self-styled poets, closet pornographers,
and sweet Max Jacob, and fat Apollinaire.

Pablo is sensitive about his stature
and takes little pleasure
in besting Toulouse-Lautrec—a sexless midget
in a top hat, as he rudely puts it.

Pablo is so jealous he won't let me work
or even leave the studio—when I went for a drink
at the Lapin à Gill he slapped me across the face,
which was a bit of a surprise. Of course
what I learned in my years modeling nine hours a day
is that I do not want to work nine hours a day,

so I try to bear Pablo's moodiness,
weeks on end when nothing but his art exists,
and give him what he wants
when he wants it.

I am hardly the most passionate of women
but men crave some essence my skin
exudes, a rank and sensual musk.
And men are fools who think with their cocks.
Anyway, I would rather be in bed than cleaning.
For a woman of my status, I say, housework is demeaning.

He rages, but my languor outlasts his machismo.
I am your mistress, not a servant, Pablo.
If you want the dishes done,
I tell him, hire a maid. And he does.

Picasso

At the Circus Medrano I laugh like a child,
I buy drinks for the clowns
at the bar that smells of sawdust, sweat, elephant shit and stale beer.

But when I paint, acrobats contort
to hollow-boned harlequins in rose-hallowed space,
five chalk fingers of a skeletal hand arrayed against the void.

Art is not documentation but transformation,
it stands apart from reality as actors against a stage set.
The painting is my creation; I will fix the terms.

Every canvas lives a double life and carries its secrets to the grave,
just as the *Burial of Casagemas* transfigures my guilt
over his suicide into silvery cumulus borrowed from El Greco.

The *Boy with a Pipe* is smoking opium
and so those mysterious, asymmetrical wreaths
emanate not from the wallpaper but his invigorated mind.

The painting wrongly called *Les Demoiselles d'Avignon* relates the
    entire history of art,
the first stepping forth like a Neolithic goddess from red cavern walls,
the next pair chiseled Hellenic odalisques burnished by
    Mediterranean light,

the final two the same, the same,
only adorned with the common masks of modernity,
thus ghastly, primeval, electric and sublime.

Apollinaire (1908)

To live in these streets is to disavow the paradise of spirits
As in Constantinople to dream of heroic eyes
Great waterfalls mighty rivers the Bosphorus full of shell-colored sails
To swim like a great poet drowning heartward
Channels and arteries crammed with ink-bloomed flowers
Attention to constant delight in inconstancy

Shiny coins in a well bespeak an impecunious boyhood
Summer rafts on blue water the coarse cries of gondoliers

Life is a death sentence
Glimmering imperative lacking syntax

All the statues sport epaulets of city pigeons
Tonsure of feathers
And boutonnieres of pigeon shit

Even the sky speaks of a future dressed in white gloves

Cloud cycles with wheels like an African mirage
Smoking omnibuses and soldiers on tired horses
The shopkeeper's treasured monotony fine-grained as rice
A parade of market girls in lace caps laughing

My cloak a rain cloud of vermin
My fine bowler hat my buttons of ivory

I smile amid their joy looking forward
To oysters and English ale
The comfort of snail-bulbs
Soft as tinsmith's butter on the gullet

Later it is evening
Stars and alcohol the City's only consorts
As I too would choose none but they to consort with
If I were Paris
Which in a manner of speaking I am

Gertrude Stein (1909)

I arose.

I arouse.   Eye *arroz*.   I arrows.

I, a rose!

Virginia Woolf: Three Fragments (1910)

i.

How much must we carry with us? Must we bear the souls of errand
boys, drovers, butchers in bloody smocks, the souls of houseflies
buzzing around kitchen windows? And the souls of flowers in shaded
gardens, what of them? And the cost to oneself, the cost inked in
green leather ledgers? How provisional our lives, propped up by
custom and social function—we need the Empire not merely to
keep ourselves surfeited with luxuries but to stay sane; if not for the
allowance of an uncle the spinster becomes a wandering lunatic, the
shopgirl a prostitute, the woodcutter abandons his children in the for-
est, etc. Cézanne's work at last has arrived in London and it becomes
clear how far behind we have fallen in imagining the modern, though
paintings seem petty in comparison to books, I confess. From the asy-
lum yard, a stone's throw away, I can hear the inmates at play—their
welcoming grunts, their adulation. Damnation, for me, would not be
madness but voicelessness. Silence. Illegibility. To scratch my glyphs
like a trained monkey, to look up at the master's baffled mouth, his
wrinkled brow, his eyes betraying fearful incomprehension.

ii.

) a tapestry woven of words
) a wishful hush
) a waterwheel, the millrace

) churning, the gears' greased conversation
) symphony of the tongue-struck

) a calling-out, a beacon, a casus belli

) o my little waterfall, awash in sympathy

) poor phlox

) sweet william and timothy

) sibilance, trance-talk, the waves' euphonic convergence

) a ticker-tape tea cozy, civilization in a jam jar

) a type a trope a trophy a trice a trace

) a caste a tribe a clan a class

) dens of lions, speckled eggs, decks of cards

) a desk set, a settee, a nest of vipers

) two steps into the darkness but no more

iii.

This world and me, this self, myself, this London,

this demi-paradise of happily breeding men, these bank vaults, these
mews, these lanes of haberdashers and umbrella makers, these gilded
motorcars—the petrol smoke of Empire—this small, cold, dismal island

with half the world in its pocket like a watch on a fob,

this England.

We cannot blame the Victorians for their strange lacunae, their
black silences, their thrift and providence and duty, their secrecy
of the self even from the self, most especially from the self. They
lacked the necessary idiom, the truth-telling machinery we take for
granted in the cinema of the psyche that has replaced the vaudeville

theater of those earlier, dustier times, those harder-working, more deeply repressed—though no less thoroughly sexualized— times. So generations evolve, correcting the obvious faults and perpetrating new ones to be reacted against by a future currently mewling and cooing in the prams of Kensington Gardens.

Mother to daughter, it passes; but it is always the father we fear,

whose needs and jealousies remain forever invisible to himself alone, damage to the hull below the waterline,

every man captain of his own catastrophe.

Picasso & Georges Braque (1911)

Picasso

As if the Inquisition had returned to torment us, as if one must
    convert or burn, everyone proclaims himself a Cubist now.
As if it were possible to adopt another's style like borrowing a studio
    or winter coat.
As if the manner of one's painting were of as little import as
    allegiance to a lover or a favorite café.

Art is not a cloakroom, it is not a religion or a social club.
There is no salvation in a new way of seeing, only a new way of
    seeing.

My new studio is in Montparnasse, where they prefer boxing to the
    circus, cocaine to wine, Russian émigrés to Gertrude Stein.
The young artists are Slavs, Americans, Polish Jews, a motley of
    high-spirited Italians better at partying than painting with
    originality,
many of them Futurists, Orphists, Simultaneists, heaven knows what
    else.

As a movement Futurism is both pretentious and pedantic, as an
    aesthetic so baldly plagiarized from Braque and myself as to be
    laughable.
A Russian, perhaps, or even an American, but what does an Italian
    know about the future?

Still I retain a fondness for Fernande, though her betrayal of me with
    a twenty-year-old gigolo from Bologna

proves her not only lazy and vain but blind to provide the excuse I
   desired to escape to the Left Bank with Eva.

Le Dôme, La Coupole—the cafés in this quartier are passable.

Of the artists, Lipchitz shows potential while Modigliani digs
   himself a memorable grave,
Léger has the rhythm of Cubism without the nuance, the frankness
   without the ethic,
and Chaim Soutine has been discovered with an infestation of
   bedbugs nesting in his abscessed ear.

Which tells you all you need to know about his painting.

heaven is daily implements
accordion chatter
of the mistral across shattered tile
& silver birds
of smoke & glue // ink & graphite

close the garden door pablo!

eye rhymes
sleek leeks & a bone // an egg
apples // wallpaper
// tambourine of signs (& plums)

....(& pears)

in a bowl of ash leaves
artery of pigment

        cane   rush   stencil

```
    e   x
  t  •  t
    x   e
```

not a marriage but a peak
we climb lashed together

I am no mountaineer // pablo says
& I: the door! first close the door
then put one foot

in front of   the other

Mao: On Childhood (1912)

I was born during the Year of the Snake,
in the province of Hunan,
first son in a prosperous farmer's household.
Not until I was fourteen did I learn the existence
of steamboats, electric lights, and other Western inventions.
Beasts were our only locomotion, and men
the cheapest of beasts to keep,
porters like files of ants
bearing loads of rice to market from our home
in the village of Shaoshan.

My father was cruel and miserly,
and I learned from an early age to hate him.
I learned that oppression begins in the cradle.
I desired always to learn, and when I was betrothed
against my will to a local girl
I refused to acknowledge her as my bride.

Deaf to my mother's sobs, I abandoned my home,
and sent my application to secondary school in the next county.
My father opposed me in this plan
but was defeated
by my willfulness, as was customary between us.

Childhood resembles a pond among mountains
on which the sky inscribes simple characters in clouds.
Do not ponder too long on the meaning
of those ideograms. A mountain stream
cannot remain impeded by fallen trees forever.
This spring, next spring, soon enough the dam will burst.
What was once a rivulet shall become a torrent.

Martha (1913)

Martha, the last passenger pigeon, died in 1914 at the Cincinnati Zoo.

Three years I've been alone here now, the last, the endling,
three years whistling in the dark since the rest of them passed,
dead and gone, even old George, who shared my perch
for a decade and lately these bars through which we glimpsed
a pale blue sky no longer bewildered by companionable wings.

Can't say I miss him much—he was a tiresome, ordinary bird,
even for our kind, and we were never flashy,
even when our billions cast the earth into shadow,
even when we darkened Ohio with the shade of a single flock.

Can't say I'll miss this cage, prison cell visited by unsightly gawkers,
when I follow George and all memory of our song has vanished
from these familiar hills and woods and gentle river valleys.
You were our perfect match, Ohio, drab, anodyne, wan but fertile.

Once we ruled the roost but now comes the turn of those sly
scurrying creatures we often laughed at from the safety of our nests.
Safety? What did we know—we were pigeons!
There was no hickory so high they could not climb to steal our eggs,
no refuge in crowds from their shotguns and nets, their poison seed
spread among the tantalizing corn rows, no number so big
they could not subtract it down to zero.
                                        No, not zero, not yet.
I've got one more winter in me and feel no rush to depart,
though God knows Cincinnati is enough like hell
that I should recognize the original if I were to happen upon it.

Farewell, Ohio, you've earned the gratitude of this unlovely dove,
last of a vanquished species. Farewell and good luck.
They are not like to treat you any kinder
beneath a sky that echoes only the longing in their hearts.

Ernest Swinton: "Mother" (1914)

The war began in August. By September it was already a platitude
that defensive technologies had far outpaced offensive—barbed
wire, trenches and pillboxes, most of all machine guns against
which the assaults of massed infantry degenerated into slaughter.
The slashing purpose of cavalry being no longer supportable by
horse and rider, a military age descended from antiquity has come
to an end. What was required was an armored vehicle capable
of destroying enemy machine guns and plowing through wire
entanglements, shell holes, and other desolations of No-Man's-
Land, which I accordingly proposed in detailed memoranda to the
Home Office and GHQ as the war's first winter commenced. "I
laugh at ideas," General Foch of the French has declared, so the
British Army's refusal to engage my revolutionary notion was no
large surprise, though one could hardly have imagined that Lord of
the Admiralty Churchill would champion the project, accordingly
dubbed "Landships," later code-named "Tanks," to deceive the
enemy into believing we were designing mobile water storage
devices fitted with the latest caterpillar tracks from American
tractors. Planning, engineering, fabrication: we did what we could,
begging money to fund development. Few listened. Progress inched
forward. It was of course our intention to save lives, to stem the
obscene slaughter on the western front—yet the mindless battles
continued, the dead beyond counting by the time the Tanks at last
were available to perform as they were intended, in numbers, over
traversable ground, with airplanes in close support, leading the
infantry forward at Cambrai. It was the resurrection of offensive
warmaking and therefore not merely the birth of modern war
but the martial image of the future, the point of the spear thrown
forward into the heart of the still fresh century. In the end the
Tanks proved their worth, and revealed their frailties, lessons taken
up by eager students whose names we would learn a generation

hence—Rommel, Patton, Guderian—though I still hearken back to the day our first Mark I prototype crawled forth, at Hatfield Park, slimed with English mud, like a huge grey mechanical slug. First of its terrible kind, we called it "Mother."

Picasso & Juan Gris (1915)

Picasso

la guerre	a	lemon
man	dolin	form
counters	form	x
x	facets	the
guitar	*ma*	*jolie*
o	live, *morte*	x
two dice	el	ements
x	*le jour*	*nal*

Juan Gris: Portrait of Pablo Picasso

pobrecito / parted porphyry

acid-etched
blind and geo /morphic

listening to radio signals / in a goldmine!
of all elements!

*

planar, palette-handed / partaking of purity

in a zinc quarry / ochre

cantilevered / subcutaneous
as many as
sixteen frames / solder & soldier-coat, *¡nuestro*

Señor!

of un / transmuted lead

Easter, 1916

A terrible beauty is born. Just before sunrise on February 21
bombardments for the German attack at Verdun commence;
two million shells are fired in five days; death is a grinding down
of obdurate surfaces, a pulverization of will, a blind slaughter
by distant artillery of helpless men huddled in freezing mud.
Death is invisible, impersonal, mechanical: the flamethrower
is introduced as a tool of destruction; phosgene gas is introduced;
airplanes, for the first time, operate in organized squadrons.
Seventy thousand men will fall each month until December.
In March, Apollinaire receives a shrapnel wound in the temple;
he is sent home to Paris to recuperate, with a hole in his skull.
For years he has beaten the drum for modern art
and now martial drums have swept everything before them—
war, the human antithesis of art; even his subversive genius
cannot reconcile the two, though seldom have death and poetry
been so intimate. Wilfred Owen is still in England,
digging practice trenches on Tavistock Square
with the Artists Rifles, within sight of Yeats's house;
completing his training he lodges above the Poetry Bookshop
and ships out in December for the "seventh hell" of the front
as a second lieutenant in the 2nd Manchester infantry.
In Zurich, Tristan Tzara edits the first issue of the journal *Dada,*
while Lenin argues that Imperialism is a final-state corollary
of Monopoly Capitalism, a contest for markets and cheap labor.
It is tempting to imagine him happening upon the Cabaret Voltaire,
stepping inside to watch the goings-on. *Da da da da da.*
How else can art represent this world's grotesque absurdity?
Jack London dies. D. W. Griffith's *Intolerance* is released.
Kirk Douglas and Gregory Peck are born. Walter Cronkite is born.
Tsutomo Yamaguchi— the only officially recognized survivor

of both the Hiroshima and Nagasaki nuclear explosions— is born.
Louis Armstrong is driving a coal wagon in New Orleans,
Margaret Sanger opens the first American birth control clinic.
Rasputin dies under mysterious circumstances in Saint Petersburg;
the tsar's control is crumbling, Revolution is imminent.
The Easter Rebellion of the Irish Republican Brotherhood
fails to inspire a popular uprising and is quickly suppressed;
James Connolly, Pádraig Pearse and a dozen other leaders
of the revolt are executed by British firing squad in Dublin.
The gears of war keep turning. Wyndham Lewis leaves BLAST
to serve as an artillery spotter at Ypres; Walter Gropius
earns an Iron Cross for valor. During the Mexican Revolution
Pancho Villa attacks and burns the town of Columbus, New Mexico;
for the next year American cavalry troops will pursue Villa,
unsuccessfully, throughout Sonora and Chihuahua.
The Battle of the Somme begins in June: advancing at a walk,
sixty thousand British soldiers fall the first day;
a million casualties before it is done, tens of thousands vanished
without a trace in the churned inferno of No-Man's-Land.
Wilfred Owen is in the front lines again in April 1917.
"I kept alive," he writes, "on brandy, fear of death,
and the glorious prospect of the cathedral in St. Quentin."
His unit attacks German machine gun posts over open ground.
They sleep on an unprotected hillside in snow for a week.
Retreating, they are gassed. Owen falls into a deep crater
and suffers a concussion; a shell, exploding near his bunk,
flings him bodily into the air. Hospitalized for shell shock,
he meets Siegfried Sassoon, begins to publish his poems,
cannot fathom the hypocrisy of politicians and churchmen
praising the righteousness of this most un-Christian of wars.
Nonetheless, he returns to his unit at the front in 1918,
where, on November 4, he is involved in a nighttime assault
on the Sambre-Oise Canal during the war's final battle.

Five days later Apollinaire succumbs to the Spanish flu epidemic,
never fully recovered from his wounds. On November 11,
bells are ringing to mark the Armistice when a telegram
arrives at the door of a mother's house outside Shrewsbury:
Wilfred Owen is dead. The war is over. *Dulce et decorum est.*

Mao: On Education (1917)

In Dongshan I read Adam Smith, Darwin, Rousseau and Locke,
and saw for the first time a map of the world.
First in my class, I was content
to imagine myself dressed in the robes of a scholar.

At eighteen I moved to the provincial capital of Changsha,
with its ancient walls and busy port on the river Xiang,
in that vicious and euphoric year
when the Manchu Emperor was opposed, civil war engaged,
and we students stood in the vanguard of the possible.

I joined the revolutionary army in Hankou,
and served for seven months, until the future
hung in the balance like an acrobat.
In the north they sow wheat, in the south rice.
Which way would China tumble?

My first love was poetry, the elegance of classical verse,
but I was moved by the vigor of the times
to study law, economics and social thought.
At the Teachers' College
I had little interest in natural history
but of all subjects the one I could not abide was life drawing.

For my final exam, I composed a simple oval,
submitted my sheet, and left.

It was an egg.

That was the only class
I ever failed.

1. Verdun

```
            h
            e
            a
w o u n d n u o w
            a
            e
            h
```

2. Spanish Flu

```
        b   b
      b        b
      b        b
   aaaaaaaaaaaaaaaa
```

I opened the window

                                                                      &

```
        &
influenza   a-a-a
                a
            ah-choo!
```

(& so adieu)

Wittgenstein: Letter to Bertrand Russell (1919)

In 1914, as the Austrian army retreated before the Russians,
while I was stuck with an engineering unit, repairing vehicles
and reading Tolstoy's version of the Gospels, I received a postcard
from a friend in Vienna, informing me that the poet Georg Trakl
was recuperating from wounds not far away, in Kraków,
and urging me to visit him at my convenience. What delight
to discover a fellow voice in the midst of war's monotony!
I struggle not to hate all those around me, and to recognize
in them some common humanity with myself.
Survival in these times, as you will understand, Russell,
can depend on having even a single real companion, a single soul
to comprehend one's ideas, one's mode of thought, one's vision.
Needless to say I rushed to the military hospital, only to discover
that Trakl had killed himself two days earlier. What misery!

In 1916 at last I received my requested transfer to the front,
where I volunteered for the most hazardous duty,
manning the forward observation post, to be certain of drawing fire.
Fear of death proved both harrowing and clarifying.
At heart we are animals, Russell. By day I was corresponding
with Frege on logic, but at night, during the Brusilov Offensive,
with the Russian artillery barrages exploding around me,
I found myself driven toward ontological inquiry.
What do I truly know about life, the world, about God?
What can be proven or derived, and via which calculus?
What means of situating oneself to receive such knowledge?
God grant me insight. Enlighten me. I am a worm.
I resemble the man in a storm, whose friends, behind their window,
cannot conceive the wild winds raging against him.

Now, as you know, I am taken prisoner by the Italians,
along with most of the Austrian army, which, in essence,
abandoned the war and surrendered en masse last autumn.
The good news is that I have at last solved all of our problems
and succeeded in completing my *Tractatus Logico-Philosophicus*.
Logic and ontology are syntactically parallel, and hereafter
no further questions remain to be answered in either realm.
I do worry, however, that my method may not be understood,
as even Frege seems unable, or unwilling, to grasp it.
Certainly your own recent writings suggest that my meaning
will pass you by completely, without lengthy explanations,
impossible unless you can somehow arrange to visit me
here, at the prisoner of war camp, in Cassino,
as I carry with me the only copy of the manuscript.

The war has changed me. Cambridge is a fond memory
but I have decided to become an elementary school teacher,
working, I hope, in the most isolated Alpine districts.
Friends in the Vatican have worked for my early release
but of course I will refuse any special considerations.
I have a rather funny anecdote to relate from the other day.
Some of the officers, one of them a reputable Viennese sculptor,
were talking of the painting by Klimt of "Fraulein Wittgenstein,"
and when I said I knew it well, being a portrait of my sister,
they fell back in amazement, having taken me for a common soldier.
It is very hard not to be understood by any single other
person in the world—the entire world, Russell.
There is a perilous loneliness in this state of affairs,
and a planetary sorrow in my soul. Yours, Ludwig.

BOOK TWO

Mao: On Conflict (1920)

Governor Tang was a strict administrator
but his methods were efficient.
Under his rule crime has disappeared in Changsha—
even dogs and chickens go about unafraid.
If 10,000 were killed, this may be considered
the cost of law and order in difficult times.
Did not General Feng execute twice as many in Nanjing?
Does not history demonstrate that the elimination
of political opponents
is both natural and inevitable?

Until this revolutionary year
I have considered the greatest contemporary thinkers
to be western humanists such as Bertrand Russell,
Henri Bergson, and John Dewey.

Now I must concede the precedence of Kropotkin and Marx
and eagerly await the translation of Lenin's writings.
The social issues I have long contested
I now understand to be economic issues at heart—
even the emancipation of women, who are less
prostitutes to their husbands, as I had imagined,
than slaves of a domestic economy.
The entire inherited burden of obedience
with which China has been laden since the days of Confucius
is a device of the ruling classes to maintain the dominance
of aristocrats and merchants, feudal warlords and corrupt officials.

What I had thought to be bindings of green bamboo
are shackles of silver, manacles of gold.

Ours is an age of conflict, bloodshed, fear and excitement.
As often before in China's history, great men
strive to make their vision dominant,
and their implement is power. The years ahead will be a test
of will, intellect and rhetorical skill, for which I am well equipped.
Only the heat of the forge can shape a blade.
From disorder comes new order. For this reason,
a long period of peace would prove unbearable to me.

Picasso & Olga Khokhlova (1921)

Olga

Señor Picasso is hardly the romantic suitor
one had imagined, though of course my girlish dreams
of troikas and Russian princes would seem
to have been irrevocably neutered
by the revolutionary Bolshevik unpleasantness at home.
Still he is a man possessed of dramatic charm

if not exactly elegance. He adores the ballet,
for which he has created many beautiful designs,
and considers Nijinsky and Massine
as nearly equal to great painters in their artistry.
He is persistent in pursuit of his desires!
On my demurral, his dark eyes radiate Spanish fire

though he understands my circumstances
and so forgives me, a bit grudgingly.
It seems one has so little upon which to rely,
in these times, except one's innocence.
Having dwelled so long in a bohemian demimonde
one can feel sure that Pablo is eager to ascend

society's ranks from such depravity, and is prepared
to keep a wife in the appropriate manner.
He appears *très chic* in evening clothes,
with freshly polished shoes and pomade in his hair
amidst the opening-night pomp and glamour
at the theater. And so we are betrothed!

I have met his dear, plump mother in Barcelona,
and his family of course approves. *Et voilà!*
Pablo's enormous fame in both Spain and Paris
promise a future of wealth and happiness—
just last month in Madrid a royal performance
was commanded by King Alfonso, a lover of the dance

though not, one surmises, a dancer in his own right.
Pablo and the King got along famously,
though Diaghilev, alas, has quarreled with Nijinsky,
and the Ballets Russes dims towards twilight.
Thus does one surrender a tutu for a trousseau,
to assume a starring role as Madame Picasso.

Picasso

Even the worst model is content
to sit for her portrait, but will the portrait
sit for the painter? A guitar resembles

a woman geometrically, cones and trapezoids
assembled upon the table's plane,
pipe, bottle, lemon, but

where is that composition situated, in space
or in the mind of the artist?
Yes, color can be symbolically expressive,

but color is color. Paulo sits happily
on his donkey whether the room is rose
or burgundy or charcoal,

as I too may be said to feel childish joy today.
Paulo smiles, the donkey is a photograph,
only the painting seeks an escape,

like a bank robber riding a golden butterfly.
Hurry, pin its wings to the canvas.
Work fast and regret nothing.

August Sander: *Citizens of the Twentieth Century* (1922)

Because time is ahistorical but our institutions
embody the formal structures of their age,
what we retrieve from his photographic folios
is an inventory of the folk, a social typology
in a world of class appellations—*Bourgeois Couple,*
Children of the Rural Proletariat, Baron von Maltitz—
a visual elegy etched in chemicals and light
for a culture arisen from medieval dreams
to become a realm of mustachioed bankers
and bespectacled revolutionaries,
a world of itinerant carpenters in silk hats,
tramps in long coats subsisting on windfall apples,
a farm girl with luxurious braids primly seated
before a pathway angled between brooding trees.

And because the history of their century
would be fire and ash, *götterdämmerung,*
his work composes a black-and-white memorial
for a society on the brink of absolute destruction,
census of the oblivious, roll call of the doomed:
blacksmiths, cobblers, millers, field hands;
page after page of farmers tan as leather,
wrinkled as the fields they plough with teamed oxen;
amateur pilots in goggles and flying scarves,
confident architects as avatars of the zeitgeist
bearing blueprints of modernist structures
never to be built or built and destroyed
in onslaught or downfall; nurses and theologians,
a leering Dadaist, an unemployed sailor
on a bridge over a canal of mule-drawn barges;
industrialists, magicians, blind children

holding hands at the asylum—everything lost,
the world alike with its representations,
image and body reduced to ruin.

Even the customs officials in brass-buttoned tunics.
Even the proud hod carrier with his brick-laden shoulders.
Even the girl with black-ribboned braids on a bench
where the narrow lane enters the woods.

Everything about her cries out from a bygone era—
her prim dress and elaborate bows,
everything but her ageless, unarchivable face.
In her hand she clutches a slim volume, a diary
or psalter or pamphlet of sentimental verse.
Her head is turned expectantly, as if waiting
for a tram to convey from the electrified city
all the cosmopolitan aspirations of modern times
but we know, as she does not, that there will come
no rescue from the direction of the future.

And the past?

Already the path behind her is disappearing
into the gloom, consumed, as in a folktale,
by the grim, insatiable shadows of the forest.

Matisse: Nice (1923)

This city resembles the bored, immodest women I paint by the dozens,
louche houris in harem pants
baring their breasts to the Mediterranean wind.

I live now on a rectangular canvas stretched between the castle and
    the harbor,
between the tawdry glamour of the gamblers risking fortunes at the
    Casino
and the cross-hatchings of the old quarter where the Niçois
hang laundry and filigreed cages for parakeets along a web of
    alleyways congested as a Moroccan souk.
Alone with the goldfish in my studio, how is it
I fail again in my intention
to visit my family in Paris, seasons becoming years,
thinking only of painting, standing at the window in my striped
    work-pajamas,
walking the streets in *sabots*
through unfelt snow, chained to the ranks of my odalisques.

My birthday passes unnoticed.
To my children I become inscrutable, unreachable.
I am fifty-three.

Last night I came across the orderly chaos of a movie being filmed,
the Director shouting through his megaphone at 1 A.M.
while firemen turned their hoses to a cold drizzle falling on a
    caravanserai of camels and horses, robed sheiks,
all the exotic machinery of their masquerade,
the strange, illusory illumination of the cinema like the light of our
    world seen through the heavy glass of a fishbowl.

Only in retrospect can the life of the artist be understood for what it is,
only in the Thousand and One Nights
of his seduction by the muse and her lush confabulations.

My father was a seed-merchant in Flanders.
My people have lived in that unlovely precinct for centuries.
From treeless fields I have come to this place of salt-stained silk and
     inarticulable sadness.

From the labor of shopkeepers and tradesmen, from the loom-toil of
     village weavers.
From grim rectitude, from thrift and vigilance.
From oyster-shell to crimson and topaz, from ashen bistre to
     sumptuary light.

From the quietude of the Middle Ages I awoke
as a flight of arrows above the plain,
as a file of crows battling northern squalls.

From dream to dream, unending.

Kafka (1924)

That people truly are as they appear, wearing hats
in the street, chewing pencils at work,
even naked in bed, in passion—that this is so
continually arouses in me
feelings of the most extreme astonishment.

*

Gravestones are teeth in the jaw
of the devouring earth, are they not?
Precious incisors, holy relics.
Thus we explain the crooked smiles
on the faces of all the angels in the paintings.

*

The way water runs through coffee grounds,
taking on new life, scorched
and exhilarated by the process, the process,

and then the coffee comes into focus,
dark as blood, transformed utterly—

if our lives could aspire to such revision,

if we could mimic the miraculous
strip of celluloid through which the projector
casts its beam of light and desire
toward the awaiting movie screen.

*

This is no fairy tale.
The man approaching from the shadows is indeed a torturer.

The mouth he seals may be mine, but the wrists
he binds with shackles, the calipers, the subtle blades—

can you not understand
it is your own flesh to be torn?

*

Every draft, every notebook, every word—
burn it all,
Max, burn everything.

Frida Kahlo: Self-Portrait Pierced by a Silver Rail (1925)

my squash blossom my rainsquall my unicorn
my quince and melon my torn garments my torment
my chalk slate my silver nitrate my metastatic *autoretratos*
my nation my hospital bed my sequestration
my thumbscrew my monkey paw my green macaw
my parrot feather my fetuses my head of lettuce
my seashell my curfew my you know who
my can my cant my revolutionary rant
my Diegos my no nos my yes yes yeses
my sister my disasters my star-crossed kisses
my hits and misses my cicatrix *y cicatrices*
my skirts and dresses my plaits and tresses
my pains my distresses my lisping *s*'s
my shyness my eyelessness my bloody messes

Rilke: *Les Saltimbanques* (1926)

Rilke's preoccupation with strolling players would develop
into a fixation on Picasso's great Saltimbanques *composition.*
Hertha Koenig, then owner of the painting, had loaned Rilke
the Munich apartment where it hung. As he sat day after day
meditating on this canvas, which epitomized the Paris he loved
and thus helped him to forget the war, Rilke embarked on one of
his most engaging elegies.

—JOHN RICHARDSON, *A LIFE OF PICASSO*

In Munich I passed an entire summer's span
with his *Saltimbanques* feeding my eyes alone,
but it was not Bavaria, or linden-lined Berlin,
or Vienna or Prague or the City of Heaven
but Paris that awoke in me, city of my own
and the century's irrecoverable youth,
saved from the Great War of man against man
but lost to the siege of time against truth.

These are no ordinary souls, Picasso's tumblers,
enacting the acrobatics of Thanatos and Eros,
moving my heart as a red pin on the battle-chart
in a war room where officers administer
plans for Armageddon. O Angel, paradise
is not this earthly flesh, but its paraphrase in art.

Fiber 66: Meet the Latest Miracle Product from DuPont (1927)

Guess what? I'm the world's first synthetic fiber!
I was conceived in a laboratory beaker
and born right here
at the DuPont refinery in Wilmington, Delaware,
but soon I'll be everywhere!
Technically, I'm a linear cold-condensation superpolymer,

and so, like latex or mastic,
I'm resinous, translucent and amazingly elastic.
Like a dinosaur hatchling at the dawn of the Jurassic
the world belongs to me—because this is the Age of Plastic.
Isn't that fantastic?
I'm built from six-carboned adipic acid

and hexamethylenediamine, so "Fiber 66" is my secret identity.
Like you, I'm a product of organic chemistry.
Wood, fabric, metal—I can be all three.
I'm the purest form of consumer friendly twentieth-century
materiality, the epitome
of corn-fed American ingenuity.

Born in 1935, after an eight-year chemical gestation,
they had a hard time christening me—Adalon,
Supraglos, Lustrol, Neosheen, Hexafil, Dulon,
Yarnamid, Wacara, Pontex, NuRay, Shimaron?
Surprise, it's me—good old Nylon!
Your pal, your buddy, your sidekick, from now on.

Edward L. Bernays (1928)

People will buy anything if you make them want it bad enough,
if you give them something to chew on, a little skin,
a little rhubarb, an elbow in the ribs. Looking back, 1928
was the true birth of the Public Relations Industry,
when Lucky Strike cigarettes decided to sell smoking to women
and hired me to create the first professional PR campaign.
I never yet met a lady who wants to look fat, so the first act
was to promote cigarettes after dinner instead of dessert,
affidavits from medical bigwigs declaring cigarettes would save you
from the dangers of eating sweets, the Ziegfeld girls
testifying that Lucky Strikes kept them svelte, so by implication
not to smoke is to be a fat-ass tub of lard, a sow, a hag.
Still, smoking was "unladylike," so to crack that stigma
we came up with the Torches of Freedom march,
modern women parading down Fifth Avenue,
stylish, good-looking gals lighting up in public
as a protest against the oppression of their sex, the outrage
of being denied the right to kill themselves with cancer
on an equal footing with men, which is when I understood
that I could change anything, given time and money,
not just consumer choices but values, habits, social taboos.
The key is to leave no fingerprints, no paper trail,
to rely on indirect action through front organizations,
photo ops with matinee idols, expert testimony, lobbying
geared toward public fears aroused by one's own scare tactics.
People will buy anything if you hook them on the narrative—
bacon and eggs as health food, the liberation of Guatemala
on behalf of the United Fruit Company, beer as a bulwark
against intemperance. Last time I saw my Austrian uncle,
the famous Doctor Freud, we walked together in the Vienna woods
discussing family matters and the application of his theories,

not yet widely known in the USA—this was 1913 and I was
still a press agent working with showgirls and vaudevillians,
coveting every column inch, pestering editors for ink,
so I understood the value of symbols and images, the power
of suggestion to shape desire, the need to ring the bells
that drive the herd—but how could I have known,
talking with Uncle Sigmund, how far his ideas would carry me,
that they'd find my book in Goebbels's personal library after the war,
that the entire country would sell itself to the highest bidder,
that the President would end up packaged and marketed
like a box of frozen peas and carrots? Listen,
Henry Ford did not invent the car but who remembers
the name of the schmuck that did?
PR is my baby, no apologies, no regrets.
I wrote the rules and chopped the trees and paved the runway,
and when Felix Frankfurter denounced me to FDR
as a "professional poisoner of the public mind"
I admired a nimble piece of wordcraft, and I still consider it
as accurate a label as any my job will ever have,
but most of all I knew we had made it to the big time.
Greatest country in the world, America.
People will buy anything.

Woody Guthrie: Rusty Bedspring Blues (1929)

My mother, Nora Belle, had long been moody and strange, but nobody
knew she was sick with the chorea, and after she burned up my
father with kerosene across his chest she was sent to the asylum for
good, and he, to recover for a year, leaving me and my brother Roy
to fend for ourselves throughout nineteen twenty-seven,

Roy signing on at the market and me jig-dancing on sidewalks and
rapping the bones for spare change,

working as needed shining shoes, polishing spittoons, picking cotton
or washing dishes at the chili palace for seventy-five cents a day,

living sometimes with friendly families in town, the Smiths, the
Prices, the Moores,

or just sleeping in haylofts and shanties, not caring what opinion was
formed of me by the good citizens of Okemah, Oklahoma, which
might as well have been the title of my very first song, the "Go
Ahead and Call Me a Tramp Blues."

Summer of nineteen twenty-eight, after school closed up, I set out on
the road the first time, hitchhiking through Houston to the Gulf
of Mexico,

following the sun-ruined roads from town to town, through fishing
camps on bayous smelling like teardrops with torn-up nets in
the branches and the lacework of fish bones and silver scales on
bleached wood where pelicans clacked their bills to those "Gulf
Coast Afternoon Rainstorm Blues,"

and the lumber and turpentine camps back up in the piney woods,
red-dirt farms poor as pellagra where I hoed figs, picked
strawberries and mustang grapes, pumping gas at crossroads
service stations,

tooting my harmonica and singing my ditties at fish fries, church
socials, railroad stations and whorehouses.

No good water, no good houses, no jobs, no prospects, East Texas
was a text in human misery, a message I was not ready at sixteen
to articulate, though anyone with eyes understood the injustice of
that poverty.

Oh, and I met a girl I called Dolores, though that was not her name,
and tasted in her hair at midnight the secret essence of the wind.

Nineteen and twenty-nine, first year of the Dust Bowl, I followed
my daddy Charley to Pampa, Texas, working as night clerk in a
flophouse of one hundred and twenty cots for oil field roughnecks,
a hardhanded collection of drillers and riggers, timber haulers
and mule skinners, boomers and roustabouts,

and the girls on the top floor priced accordingly at two dollars a
throw, plus a quarter for the bed, hence the all-night serenade we
took to calling the "Rusty Bedspring Blues."

When the bunkhouse closed I worked at Shorty Harris's drugstore,
sweeping, hauling, tidying the shelves, jerking sodas up front
while he poured corn liquor and Jamaica Ginger for parched
souls in the back room.

That's how it went—I dropped out of high school, got fired, got
hired, took things as they came, time wheeled past, until one day
I found a dust-covered guitar in the back of the store, polished
and tuned it, and set about learning to play.

Matisse: Tahiti (1930)

If I were young again I would forgo Tahiti and move to America to
    begin a new life in New York, a city both human and classical in
    its geometric modernity,
as I have discovered much too late, on my passage to the Pacific.
Nonetheless I pay homage to the lovely Polynesian women and tour
    the scenery dutifully.
I search out Gauguin's son, Émile, living the life of a fisherman,
with no wish for European ways and a contentment unknown to his
    father.
They are filming a movie here, *Tabu,* and its directors, F. W. Murnau
    and Robert Flaherty,
invite me to live for a week in their camp on an idyllic cove
more lovely than any I have seen before.

Still I find myself eager to depart for the outer islands,
the far Tuamotus, eager to escape
Papeete with its film of dust and colonial snobbery.

For three years I have painted nothing at all.
I have abandoned my wife
on her sickbed to travel halfway around the globe in search of what—
jungle flowers, an exotic cast of light?
Why does my heart remain loyal to art alone?

My dearest Amélie, let me tell you about the Tuamotus: night is a
    wash of stars in ash-blue ether,
dawn the rustle of trade winds, glitter of flying fish at the horizon.
Days, I swim in the lagoon amidst marvelous creatures of
    preposterous vividness,

sea horses, anemones, plumed aquatic ferns.

Imagine a life stripped clean of every artifice, nothing but a small
     house on white sand amid coconut palms,
and all of it, everything, subordinated to those vast, borderless fields
     of color—

the sky and the sea.

It would require a new medium to equal their purity,
and at this age I doubt myself capable
of more than these sketches of tropical foliage, shapes and notations
toward a project I sense at the furthest horizon
of consciousness,

                    a voyage

                         to the outer islands within

          the far Tuamotus of myself

                    moon-stroked atolls
               across an endless gulf of molten gold

                                   oarless
                                        brushless

                         a voyage

               undertaken without promise
     of safe passage
                         or realistic hope

          of return

Mao: On Patience (1931)

Sick with malaria, I withdraw from the clamor
of disputatious cadres
to live in a bamboo pavilion with He Zizhen,
my revolutionary companion,
who has surrendered our newborn daughter
to be raised by peasants. A model comrade, she would not
saddle the Party with an infant's needs.

Word of my wife's execution in Changsha has reached me,
and my youngest son dead, in hiding, of dysentery.
Nationalist troops have pillaged
my home village and desecrated my parents' graves.
But I have long purified myself of any attachment
which might belie the Revolution.
Who can blame a river
for the stones it tumbles smooth?
Here, I bathe in a basin on the moss-covered floor
of a cave above three ancient pagodas.
I take time, in the evenings, to inscribe the poems
I have jotted down on horseback
throughout these many months of struggle.

Returned from Moscow, the young men of the Party
exalt in the examples of Lenin and Stalin
and find me an impediment to their stratagems.
I am accused of "mistaken work methods"
but not of "patriarchal tendencies."
I am accused of a "roving bandit ideology"
but not of "right opportunism."

Running dogs, Mensheviks, bourgeois revanchists,
mountaintop-ists and closed-doorists—

life has become a contest of euphemisms,

and it is essential to win this taxonomic battle
by which future categories of enmity shall be fixed,
so that our mistakes, if any are detected,
shall be defined only as "errors in terminology."
High on a hill overlooking rough forest
I have named my new home "The Hall of the Wealth of Books."
Here, like a scholar of old, I wait
for the latest intrigues against me to play out.
Like a wise farmer, I will sow patiently.
I will husband my strength,
studying the weaknesses of those who oppose me.

It is better to burn 100 acres of grain
than to let a single snake escape the fire.

Zora Neale Hurston: Farmyard Hymns (1932)

God made mules
    and He made men,
maybe God should
    try again.

God made chickens
    cheep and squawk,
foolish creatures
    shush your talk.

God made roosters
    crow and preen,
stupidest birds
    I've ever seen.

Bacon from the sow,
    ham from the boar,
is that what God
    made piglets for?

God made horses
    strong and fast—
who cracks the whip,
    who wields the lash?

God made us,
    for good or ill,
I wonder
    is He happy still?

Frida Kahlo: Self-Portrait with Hand-Mirror and Retablo of Leon Trotsky (1933)

my canvas my prickly cactus my pickaxe
my accident my bus ride my all mixed-up insides
my androgyny my lost progeny my petite bourgeoisie
my bloodworm my cauls my sack of penny nails
my hammer and sickle my tinsmith my pictoglyphs
my disease my pliancy my splintered bones
my pelvis my Coyoacán my womb my home
my white light my Blue House my red red flag
my workers' protest my clenched fist my amanuensis
my shark my shadow my heart of darkness
my lovers and letters my his and my hers
my transfusions my transformations my testimony
my reflection my being my agony
my me my me my me

Picasso (1934)

Spain and women: they bleed,
they argue and protest,
they stink of camphor and the sea.

Yet I cannot live beyond their shadows.
I cannot create my art
without their elemental ore.

I quarry them. I gore them.
I rage against their flags and lances.
I am the bull—certainly, I am the bull.

But I am also the matador.

Orson Welles: The Stage (1935)

Empty theater, New York City.

WELLES

What lasts, what endures, as Shakespeare knew, is this:
the story of a life. No more, no less.
The stage is dark, the screen a blank, and then:
let there be light, up with the floods, the cans,
the scoops, the luminaires and follow spots,
beam from an old projector reaching out
like the mind, like the dawn, in the beginning was
the word, spoken by me, of course. Who else?

Cast against type, I stand outside of time,
forger of destinies, smelter of ore,
my voice like storm-wind swelling every sail.
For I am neither Lear nor Harry Lime
nor Charlie Kane, but he who tells the tale.
Fate's chime, destiny's roar. The narrator.

Fade to black.

Woody Guthrie: Come to Nothing Blues (1936)

By nineteen thirty-four I had married a local gal of sixteen years
    named Mary Jennings and settled down in a whitewashed
    shotgun shack behind her parents' house with our little baby
    daughter Gwendolyn.

For some time I'd been playing with the Corncob Trio weekends at
    Flaherty's Barn or the Willard Club, and had grown proficient
    not only on harmonica but the spoons and standard drum kit,
    guitar and mandolin, double bass, and could even scratch a tune
    on fiddle and warble a few notes of saxophone.

Weekly we appeared for fifteen minutes on the KPDN Breakfast
    Club broadcasting across the Texas Panhandle.

On the side I had a family trio with my Uncle Jeff and Aunt Allene,
    and one time we signed up with a traveling tent show supporting
    some Kansas City chorus girls with magic tricks and my
    cornpone palaver and pontification between sets but it didn't
    come to nothing at all,

which was about what most folks had in their pockets those years,
    which is how I commenced to hanging with the hoboes again,
    singing the "Come to Nothing Blues."

Nineteen thirty-five the dust rose up and buried Pampa, Texas, like
    the Red Sea swallowed Pharaoh's army.

Many thought it was the end-time come instead of black Kansas
    topsoil blown off hard-scratch farms a mile high, and that year
    I took to the superstition business to feed my family, reading

fortunes and healing by touch, offering lessons in telepathy,
   clairvoyance and the ciphering of dreams.

Faith healing mixed belief and money about like wildcatting for oil or
   anything else in Capitalism's kingdom, and so they paid what they
   could in nickels and dimes, sometimes a greenback dollar bill or
   a sack of chicken feed, once a red rooster and some jars of garden
   vegetables, which is when I took up the "Pickled Beets Blues."

Nineteen thirty-six, nineteen thirty-seven, what can you say about
   those rock-bottom years of the Depression?

Pampa was nothing but a load of sorry shacks abandoned by the
   boom to dust devils, oil derricks running right up to Main Street
   and carbon black refineries spewing acrid smoke, how could I
   feel sorry about leaving that mess, or my pregnant wife and child,
   with no solid income or aptitude for fatherhood?

So I hit out of town hitching west in a snowstorm, across New
   Mexico along Route 66, then riding the rails from Deming to
   Tucson, all kinds of fellows on the road, bindle stiffs and tramps
   and vagrants, men looking for any job of work,

and I had my share of easy riders and snug reefer cars, of railyard
   bulls and hobo jungles, sleeping under bridges wrapped in
   newspaper, door-to-door looking for food, on the bum, dead
   hungry,

and I hobbled through Glendale, Bakersfield and Fresno, drifted
   through the old glittering Sierras where the gold once was, waited
   in line with five thousand other fools for a dam-building job in
   Redding,

and finally come down to Los Angeles where I took what work they
had, hammering roof shingles and playing guitar in saloons
full of Okies, drinking away our homesick sorrows with the
"Lonesome L.A. County Blues."

Guernica (1937)

The canvas that yawns against a wall as blank as Guernica.
The hand that guides the brush that seeks a form.
The name of the town toward which the bombers dove: Guernica.
Cattle on green hillsides, sheep in flocks above Guernica.
a wall a city a ruin a trope a painting
For the fist and sickle, for the brotherhood of the republic: *Guernica*.
Against the triumph of lies, against the darkness: *Guernica*.
What painter, what artist, what other man than I, Picasso,
could create such a work, duly signed by my hand: *Picasso*.
As for Spain, as for politics, I have stood mute until Guernica,
watching from the safety of exile the tragedy of civil war.
Now, with paints and brushes, I march to war.

a flag a tyrant a lamp the eye of god a war
The name the lightning burns into our hearts: Guernica.
Let it stand as admonition and animadversion to all war.
Let it serve as totem and reproof to the idiocy of war
as the painting I so name bears witness to its modern form,
to Franco's savagery, the death of innocents, to war
in its ruthless, mechanical guise, twentieth century war, total war.
Against the bombs of the Fascists I counterpose my painting.
Against the destruction of Spain and its people, let this painting
embody the tribute and testament of Pablo Picasso.
The name of the matador and the name of the bull: Picasso.

The name of the Minotaur, the name of the tauromachist: Picasso.
The name of the enemy and his implement: war.
Against which, like the thunderbolts of Zeus, Picasso
hurls paint against canvas, creation against death: *¡yo, Picasso!*
From the blue sky, by the hundreds, bombs falling on Guernica.
oil paint the eye of god a sword a scream Picasso

a candle   a memory   a dream   the world in flames   Picasso
Mothers bearing dead children are anguish given form.
Stink of burned flesh and wool is obliteration in animal form.
In the eye of the bull, in the scream of the horse: Picasso.
In art there can be no compromise; only while painting
can I perceive what transcends the historical act of painting.

a lance   a banner   a template   an annunciation   a painting
A brush is a weapon of vengeance in the hand of Picasso,
to strike down death-merchants, haters of modern painting,
Franco, Mussolini, Hitler with his sentimental flower paintings.
"If cities are destroyed from the air, the enemy cannot carry on the war.
The annihilation of Guernica resembles a victorious painting
by an old master, not this infantile, degenerate painting."
From failure, from breakage, from silence, from loss: *Guernica.*
The name of the dove in the burning dovecote: Guernica.
a vision   a wound   a flame   a teardrop   a painting
With pencil, with chalk, with a brush I shall seek its form—
with my hands I shall remodel what tyranny deforms.

As for Spain, lost to medieval slumber, to a violent form
of self-abnegation, like an apparition from a Goya painting
she sinks again into the darkness. Power is a form
of narcissism; totalitarianism corrupts even as it informs
those who destroy and those who create, both Franco and Picasso.
In a century to which devastation has given its true form
Guernica is an elemental dispensation, a document formed
in the name of humanity to denounce the nightmare of war.
Against chaos, against ignorance, against all future war
a brush moves across canvas and truth takes the form
of Leningrad, of Nanking, of Hiroshima, of Guernica.
The name of the burning world is Guernica.

a vigil   a vessel   a fist   a pyre   a form
a plume   a banner   a vision   a trope   a painting
a veil   a scream   a wound   the world in flames   Picasso
a tyrant   an elegy   a lamp   a dove   a war
a dream   a ruin   a teardrop   the eye of god   Guernica

Mao: On the Long March and Protracted War (1938)

For two years, exiled from military leadership by my rivals,
I issued petty regulations
and promulgated land reform in the soviet base area,
amid the remote hill country of Jiangxi and Fujian.
Rules for farm ponds, for fallow land, for bamboo groves.
Proclamations urging the farmers
"to carry out the spring vegetable planting with fervor."
My brother Zemin produced a currency
stenciled with Lenin's likeness on crude grass paper
we forced upon the local landlords in exchange for their hoarded silver,
while in the cities, we are told, people cart inflated money
to market in wheelbarrows.
What buys three eggs in the morning
at sunset purchases only one.

Encircled by the Nationalists, besieged, we retreated
into the desolate mountains of Guizhou,
across far Yunnan, in the shadows of the Himalayas.
Harassed at every turn by warlords and enemy forces,
still, how could I not feel joy to be reunited with the Red Army,
to be vindicated in my strategy and recalled
to my position of leadership in the Party apparatus?
If the enemies' troops climb the ridge behind us,
I reflect on the inevitability of the defeat of feudalism.
If their airplanes appear in the sky
I recall the great poets of the Tang dynasty,
Li Bai and Du Fu,
whose words descend across 1,000 years of history,
from human mouth to human ear,
from heart to heart.
Bullets cannot kill such truths.

Forty-one years old, my only possessions
two blankets, an overcoat,
a broken umbrella, and a bundle of books.

In our haste to escape, our beloved son, Xiao Mao,
was left behind with local peasants, to be lost forever,
and then, amid the night calls of wild geese,
He Zizhen gave birth once more in her litter carried by soldiers,
a daughter we did not bother to name in our worry
to catch up with our comrades, retreating in small boats
by moonlight across the River of Golden Sand.

Such was the suffering of the Long March,
after which came the invasion of the Japanese,
militaristic dwarfs from the Land of the Grey Dragon.
The Party's new sanctuary was established in the far northwest,
at Yan'an, where turbaned Moslem cavalry patrol the steppe,
and camel trains arrive at the West Gate
from the fastnesses of Central Asia as they have for centuries,
and the market is always full of peddlers and good vegetables,
Mongolian herders come to trade ponies and furs,
woodcutters wheeling oxcarts of fresh-sawn boards
smelling of spring grass, herbalists proffering
jars of powdered lion's teeth.

There He Zizhen abandoned our marriage bed
and neither threat nor flattery could coax her back.

New enemies assail us, yet the Red Army endures.

Their blood is my ink, their weapons
the pen and brush of my poetry,
their triumphs great odes to the Chinese soul.

Yet the goal is not victory in this or that battle
but the realization of the Revolution
and so the deaths of soldiers, officers, entire regiments,
even the sacrifice of Party leaders, remain irrelevant.
Those who most loudly protest their loyalty
often tolerate the most severe tortures
but confession is inevitable and mercy a bourgeois affectation.

We must mobilize the great sea of the people
in which to allow the enemy,
swimming far from shore, to drown.
So the path of Revolution gains clarity
even as the nature of women continues to elude me.

The tigress is a fierce and graceful animal
but do not free her from the cage
unless you know which way she will leap.

The Atomic Clock (1939)

The clock is ticking. The century is getting old, the century
is coming apart at the seams. Eagle-taloned century,
century of steel & Kodachrome, of caesium-137 & Zyklon B.
In January the achievement of nuclear fission is confirmed
in *Naturwissenschaften* magazine. In August Einstein
and Leo Szilard post their urgent request to President Roosevelt
to develop atomic weapons in advance of the Nazis.
The Manhattan Project is born; the atomic clock has been wound;
the future, from now on, will be measured in half-lives.
Nationalist troops enter Madrid, the Spanish Republic collapses,
Franco will control the country until his death in 1975.
The Grapes of Wrath is published, *Mein Kampf* is published.
William Butler Yeats dies, Seamus Heaney is born.
Nylon stockings go on sale, Siam becomes Thailand.
Hollywood's Golden Age reaches its apogee with
The Wizard of Oz, Stagecoach & *Mr. Smith Goes to Washington.*
Martin Luther King Jr. sings with his church choir
at the Atlanta premiere of *Gone With the Wind*; he is ten.
Billie Holiday records "Strange Fruit" for Commodore Records.
Charlie Parker rides a freight train from Kansas City to Chicago
and then to New York but fails to land a steady gig,
washing dishes midnight to eight at Jimmy's Chicken Shack
in Harlem; *bebop* is not yet a term in the jazz lexicon.
Francis Ford Coppola is born. RKO Pictures signs the boy wonder,
Orson Welles, to Hollywood's most lucrative contract
then turns down his peculiar adaptation of *Heart of Darkness*;
Herman Mankiewicz is dispatched to Victorville to write *Citizen Kane.*
The movie's release in 1941 will be overshadowed by Pearl Harbor
and William Randolph Hearst's vitriolic publicity attacks.
Mankiewicz dies in 1953, on the same day as Joseph Stalin.
Century of invention, immiseration, liberation & terror,

century of cube & sphere, of Speer and Le Corbusier,
of Mississippi juke joints and Weimar cabarets.
Ernest Hemingway is drinking rum in Havana,
Gandhi is fasting against British rule in Gujarat,
from his jail cell Nazim Hikmet writes poems about Istanbul
and hazelnuts and joy and beautiful women, about
my miserable, shameful century, my daring, great, heroic century.
William Eggleston is born. Ansel Adams photographs Yosemite,
the moon has not yet risen over Hernandez, New Mexico.
Neil Armstrong is a nine-year-old Cub Scout in Ohio.
Elvis Presley is five, alone with his mama in Tupelo, Mississippi,
while his daddy Vernon serves eight months in county jail.
John Lennon will be born next year, Bob Dylan the year after.
Rock and roll is not a term in any cultural dictionary.
There are no cultural dictionaries, except perhaps the notebooks
of Walter Benjamin, cornered now by Hitler's shadow,
abandoned, in his final hour, by the angel of history.
"As flowers turn toward the sun," he writes in his last essay,
"by dint of a secret heliotropism the past strives to turn
toward that sun which is rising in the sky of history."
Century of wraiths & indeterminacy, century of jackals
& executioners, thirty thousand in a day at Babi Yar.
"Nothing which has ever happened should be regarded as lost
for history," Benjamin writes as the darkness closes in.
He, "the last European," will survive the year, but barely,
contemplating the ruins of the civilization he exalted.
Hitler invades Poland, Stalin invades Finland,
Italy invades Albania and King Zog—name like a golem
from some long-forgotten fable—King Zog flees into exile.
Every truth, every quotation, every aesthetic certainty,
every meticulously harvested grain of cultural knowledge
is torn from Benjamin's grasp by the whirlwind.
"This storm," he writes, "is what we call progress."

BOOK THREE

Virginia Woolf: Four Fragments (1940)

The way a terrier's ear flops over when scratched,
dogs and old men walking country lanes,
children catching moths with treacle—

                       this is England,
flowers turning towards the sun,
great milky English flowers in Charles Darwin's garden.

It was Darwin who decoded the murals of the great temple
at last, gospels and vedas of discredited holy men.
Religion and its inadequacies: an umbrella shorn of fabric.
Class and its entitlements: a skeleton cleansed by maggots.
The humiliation of servants—the pathetic hypocrisy
of our co-dependency—our helplessness and their servility,
heaped coal bins and larders full of geese and tins
while the poor the poor the hanged
the Irish . . .

               Often the beauty of the countryside seizes me
like a deluge—osier thickets along the riverbank,
bare branches of an apple tree against the sky.

Sometimes I wonder what it would be like to belong
to the clouds, to belong to the citizenry of the sea
instead of this islanded, oddly inward people.

A thunderhead over the green waters
of the North Atlantic.

               A prawn, a jellyfish, a whale.

*

War, war, war—again and always, the wearisome war of existence,
and then the German bombs, and then our dull, internal British wars—
against art and culture, against freedom, against women.

In the war of myself against myself the battle goes rather poorly.

No reinforcements to the trenches, no reserves to plug the line.
Leonard is distracted and one must seize the initiative while
    opportunity offers.

Into the breach, boys, this time it shall be all or nothing!

*

Planes overhead quite often these days—three raiders came in
barely above the trees, the swastikas clearly visible; we were playing
bowls on the lawn and dove for cover beneath the hedge. And the
other week one of them shot down, a tower of smoke arising from
the meadows along the river; in Lewes the enraged townsfolk
crushed the skulls of four dead German flyers in the mud, or so they
say in the village. Invasion is expected any moment. News comes
by radio and it is all quite awful. James Joyce has died: we were
the same age precisely. Dr. Freud as well, several months past—I
recall our conversation in Hampstead two years ago, how sickly he
seemed, how exhausted. When he spoke of his escape from Austria
I recalled driving through Germany with Leonard in 1935, coming
into one city or another on an afternoon when Reichsmarschall
Goering was anticipated, the roadway lined for miles with people
offering the Nazi salute as we passed in our motorcar, thinking
we might be he—we, a Jew and a woman writer, liberal British
aesthetes—so becoming aware of what Fascism really meant and
that our lives might be in actual danger (not that we cared), but
saved from implicit violence by the vast delight the people took in
Mitzi, our marmoset, the crowd's deranged intensity pivoting in an

instant from raving nationalism to oafish delight at the glimpse of a capering monkey. The house in Tavistock Square has been bombed and all the sodden papers are here with us now, most of our earthly possessions destroyed. Thank heaven one does not really care, in the end, about earthly possessions. Guns and bombs, barbarity, and then Persian rugs amidst the rubble. Civilization like a bandage pasted on a bleeding carcass. Freud's thinking about the savagery of human nature is quite profound and I regret not having read his works more fully until this late moment. At the end of our conversation he gave me, with great politesse, a single blossoming narcissus.

*

> To oppose the gleaming armies of men
> what have we been vouchsafed
> but the pencil nibs of schoolgirls,
> the knitting needles of grandmothers?
>
> To oppose the sea, what can we muster
> but a handful of useless metaphors—
> turn the tide, swim against the current—
> sandcastles against a coming flood.
>
> To oppose the body what have I got
> but pockets full of stones?

Woody Guthrie: Twentieth-Century Blues (1941)

Los Angeles in nineteen thirty-eight was a city I never did see the
  like of again for violet-hued beauty and thirsty-sapling sprawl,

sugar-rich colors unlike the sad and tattered country left behind,

smell of soil and ocean fog and orange blossoms, miles of high-rise
  banks and displaced plainsmen looking for a slice of paradise, a
  new-hatched metropolis far-spread from coastline to hills and up
  the sides of canyons and back again,

a city of automobiles and hungry desperation and westward-looking
  American hope run smack into the cold blue waters of the Pacific.

By this time I was a bit of a local radio star, partnered up first with
  my cousin Jack, a fancy-dan cowboy and western singer.

We broke the bank for a while at seventy-five dollars a week playing
  XELO out of Tia Juana, Mexico, whose unregulated border
  transmitter blasted our music so far and wide my wife could pick
  it up some nights back in Texas,

a rosy-spectacled life until I grew restless with success and bored of
  sticking in one place and hit the rails again, headed north up the
  Central Valley, following the call of those "Tired of Easy Pickings
  Blues."

The famous Hooverville among oak groves along the Sacramento
  River is where the scales fell from my eyes.

Suddenly I understood that these hungry and homeless Okies and
  Arkies dying of typhoid and smallpox, infected with rickets and

ringworm, that these were not just fine people but my brothers
and sisters, and that my duty was to speak on their behalf,

and that the fight for social justice was a political struggle and music
could be a lethal weapon in that war,

and while I never did join the Communist Party, and I would upon
hearing the words *dialectical materialism* fall into a deep and
restful slumber, I did sing those "Fellow Traveler Blues" and walked
that road so far as it led towards equality for the working class.

I suppose about as much happened to me in nineteen thirty-nine and
forty as is reasonable for any single lifetime—

battling vigilantes in the Kern County cotton patch and recording
my songs at the Library of Congress, writing a column in the
Daily Worker and putting out my own record album on RCA
Victor, meeting John Steinbeck and a bunch of movie stars and
stewing in the Reno County jail on a vagrancy charge,

and when I arrived in New York City after nearly freezing to death
during the worst winter of snow in forty years it was only a
matter of months before I hit the big time as a regular on the
major CBS radio shows, singing songs with Pete Seeger and
Huddie Ledbetter, making more money than I ever dreamed,

but wouldn't you figure that no measure of it left me satisfied, and
nothing in New York or Washington scratched the itch I felt, so
I packed my family into a dinged-up Plymouth and headed out
once again for California.

Nineteen forty-one was the year I learned to sing the "Top to
Bottom Blues" for real and true, drunk and depressed, tossing
beer bottles through the windows of my own rented house in

Pasadena, stirring up the dark water I always knew was in me,
the troubled soul that hooted like a barn owl so many nights,

when out of the blue the Department of the Interior hired me to come
up to Oregon and write some songs about the Grand Coulee Dam
they were building five hundred and fifty feet tall across the
mighty Columbia River

in that magnificent country of apples and wheat and salmon,
everything pale green and tan and silver,

and the boys getting paychecks off honest construction work, and the
local towns ready to hook into the electricity it would generate, and
the irrigation that would make the scrubland blossom so maybe
even those dusty migrants might someday settle here to farm.

Even after the finance company repossessed my car it was almost
enough to make me believe in our government, enough to
convince me that FDR was doing for the American people in fact
what Communism only claimed to do in fiction,

though I never did set eyes on Joe Stalin or the pie-in-the-sky
paradise of the Soviet Union.

Anyhow, they paid me two hundred and sixty-six dollars for the
month, and I wrote them twenty-six songs, and with all that
happened afterwards—

going to war and getting torpedoed on a merchant marine not once but
twice, years of Red hunts and Joe McCarthy, leaving one family
and starting another, writing *Bound for Glory*, cutting records,

just trying to keep my head above water while singing those
pernicious "Twentieth-Century Blues"—

with all that happened I didn't often think back upon the Coulee
    Dam until the government issued me a citation in nineteen sixty-
    four *in recognition of the fine work you have done to make our*
    people aware of their heritage and their land,

by which time I'd been living mostly in the Brooklyn State Hospital
    for a dozen years,

wasting away with Huntington's disease, which my mother died
    of and passed to me in her genes, and I passed along to my
    daughters, Gwendolyn and Sue, and young Bill killed in a car
    crash, Cathy in a fire, of my eight children only three escaped the
    curse of an early death,

and only Arlo taking up music, and only Jack Eliott and young
    Bobby Zimmerman come to play for me,

and of all the thousands of songs I wrote I do believe those Columbia
    River tunes were among my finest, which on the one hand
    demonstrates the continuing exploitation of the workingman, but
    on the other constitutes the best value Uncle Sam has ever got for
    his money.

Guadalcanal (1942)

*In his diary, Second Lieutenant Yasuo Ko'o, color bearer of the
124th Infantry, Japanese Imperial Army, recorded an unfailing
formula with which he calibrated the life expectancy of his
fellows in the last days of 1942:*

> *Those who can stand—30 days*
> *Those who can sit up—3 weeks*
> *Those who cannot sit up—1 week*
> *Those who urinate lying down—3 days*
> *Those who have stopped speaking—2 days*
> *Those who have stopped blinking—tomorrow*
>
> —RICHARD B. FRANK, *GUADALCANAL*

Awakened from dreams of rice cakes and candy
by a small frog jumping onto my face.
These creatures are known to be poisonous,
else we would certainly eat them,
if any of us remain strong enough to catch one.

Not Bashō's frog, this strange citizen of the jungle—
watching his slim body swell with each breath
what I feel is not curiosity but envy.

When I climb to my feet my head swims
as if drunk on New Year's whiskey,
I hold to a tree hoping these currents will subside
but there is no respite from this symptom,
hardly the worst of our afflictions.

These rugged cliffs resemble ink drawings
by some ancient Chinese master.

Was it another lifetime in which I sat sketching
mountains along the Kikuchi River?
Yet the discipline of tanka, I discover, perseveres
even in the face of starvation and disease.

> Gentle brother frog,
> > your jungle shows no mercy
> to weary soldiers
> > fighting for the Emperor
> > so far from Fujiyama!

Images sustain me as I walk, passing before my eyes
and flowing in memory as in a dream—
clam-diggers in the shallows of the Inland Sea,
kites shaped like bees and carp above my native village,
the ocean a swath of blue silk printed with golden flowers—
until I am summoned back by hunger pangs,
by the fetor of death here on Starvation Island.

Yesterday we dug up buds of areca palms
but there is no nourishment in their fiber
and it is weeks since we have seen a grain of rice.
Salt—my body cries out for it and I vow
to drink a mouthful of seawater
should I survive to see the ocean once again.

Furukama, Nonoyama, Kawai, Takagi—
these men we left behind yesterday, too weak to walk.
Goro attempted suicide; his wound festers,
soon he will embrace the peace he sought.

Long ago we abandoned our steel helmets,
rifles, gas masks, binoculars—skin and bones,
even the strap of an empty canteen causes agony.

Our last grenade we threw into the river,
greedily devouring the small silver fish
killed in the blast, bones boiled with wild potato vines
as soup the next morning, our final meal,
how many days past, how many?

Today I bury my pistol in a sandy bank,
keeping only my katana as final recourse.

When we come to a bridge strongly built
of hewn logs by our naval engineers
we are so weak that many men fall off.
I tumble into chest-deep water,
struggle through the current, holding fast.

Beneath a large tree on the far shore
we discover the engineers—
dead of starvation, decomposing,
consumed by the pervasive and intolerable rot.

Uemara can walk no further. I assure him
the relief party is on its way to this very bridge.
Do not leave this spot, Uemara,
you will be first to receive the rice
and canned beef as they come up the trail!

Some of the men grumble at his good fortune,
calling back as they resume the march.
Tell them which way we went, Uemara!
Don't let them forget about us, Uemara!

Of course there is no relief party—
the transports have been intercepted
and sunk by American warplanes.

All that can sustain us now is duty,
divine fortune and the will to survive.

> Starvation Island:
> as our ships drew near we cheered
> the sight of your shores—
> how few will watch them vanish,
> bright with moonlight, sailing home.

Picasso & Dora Maar (1943)

Women want me as much as I want them.
They desire my money, my brio, my fame,
and I desire their cunts as portals to eternity.
So what if they fought each other for me?

Men fight for women every day, they kill,
like Greeks and Trojans, for sheer beauty.
So what if Marie-Thérèse and Dora Maar do battle?
Love is truest when tested by jealousy.

At any rate Dora Maar was a Kafkaesque figure—
whenever I found a water stain on her walls
I worked it with fine pencil strokes until it resembled
a bug of some sort. In this way I transformed

her apartment to a bestiary, or an insect zoo.
In this way I changed her, too.

*

Four decades I have lived among the French
as a peasant in a shearling coat
wanders a beach of oblivious sunbathers.

So ill prepared are they for tragedy,
so little do they know of loss, so small
sorrow's claim on their imagination.

And now, uniform winter upon all of Europe,
Catalans, Normans, Slavs and Walloons
subsumed to unvarying, iron-taloned grey.

Look at my little tomato plant,
withering forth a crooked yellow arm,
a crown of leaves, a tassel of fruit.

Poor Paris, how I pity and depend upon it.
But I trace my lineage to Altamira and Lascaux.
I spring from cave walls and am content.

Joseph Goebbels (1944)

Propaganda is how the gods first spoke to us,
in talismans and entrails, in searchlights
inscribing their emblems upon a starry sky.

As in ancient days, instinct overrules reason,
therefore speak not to the head but the gut,
to the rough cud of hatred chewed by the mob.

Speak to fear, envy, anger, to the throng
before whose destructive machinery
one stands humbled, dumb with gratitude.

Argue in chisel-strokes and hammer blows.
Attend to symbols, language as bloody handprint.
Subordinate light at all times to shadow.

For it is not truth but myth that matters,
not the man but the image that inspires,
not history but legend that shall endure.

Speer may have built the Führer's beloved
autobahns and *Sportpalasts*
but I have constructed the Führer.

I am the altar and he the guttering candle,
I the stone, the strop, the scabbard,
he the sword for which my heart hungers.

Hiroshima (1945)

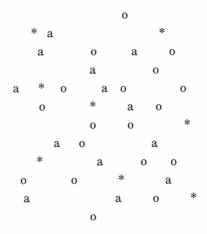

o

*

a

o

o

o

o

*

o

a

o

a

o

a

*

*

a

a

o

*

o

o

*

o

*

102

Matisse: Nice (1946)

My doctor compares my body to a crystal vase
weighted with a ballast of gravel
and so liable, with any shake, or lurch, or rattle, to shatter.

Each of the last four years he has predicted would be my last, yet
   here I am.

Fragile, yes, but how could I survive without the clarity of that vessel,
   the beauty of the tulip stems, their greed to suck the water dry?
How could I survive without Lydia to nurse me, whose name my
   wife refuses to utter or acknowledge?
When the surgeons cut and spliced my body,
when my daughter was seized by the Gestapo for her work with the
   Resistance, my beloved Marguerite,
the only one who understood the courage of my isolation,
how then could I survive, how then?

With the end of the war, color movies have arrived from America
and I have sought to imagine them as a form of painting with pure light,
as my paper-cuttings are extractions of undiluted color,
but there is so little artistry in film, so little lyrical expression,
as if we had returned to an era of studio caricature and academic
   portraits,
as if poetry did not exist, or myth,
only bedroom farce and sentimental drama.

When, against all hope, Marguerite returned after the Liberation
she came to me and, for days and nights, nonstop, replayed scenes of
   her interrogation by the Nazis,
immersion in ice-cold water, hanging by the wrists,
beatings with fists, whips, rods.

What is it to live? I ask. What is it to feel pain?
What is it to command one's muscles to torture a fellow being?
What is it to possess a body, to govern a pair of eyes, to taste an
    orange freshly broken from the branch?

Rembrandt was abandoned in old age, as am I,
alone with my private cinema
pinned to the walls, seeking resonance, contrast, balance, sequence.

The spirit, too, can be broken,
but death's embrace has made me whole,
freed me from constraint, and I work at last uninhibited
by critics and rivals, patrons and family.

People wish to partake of art as if it were pasteurized milk,
without mud and flies and shit,
but great art is the product of torment.

This is the primal struggle: to make art.
This is the passion of human existence: to endure.

Wittgenstein: Letter to Karl Popper (1947)

Herr Professor Doktor Popper, it has become apparent,
in regards to our disagreement during your lecture
last year before the Moral Science Club at Cambridge,
that an explanation of my actions is warranted.
Having had the opportunity to study your writings
I now confirm that they stand proof of a lethargic mind
preoccupied with trivia at the expense of reason and logic.
Your terms and propositions are themselves nonsensical,
a simulacrum of meaningful speech akin to the babble of apes.
Do you know the London Zoo? I recommend it.
Ethics, justice, morality: such terms must be addressed
from first causes; what can be stated or understood
about human existence; what it is to live; how we know
what we know and what may be asserted within language.

Undoubtedly totalitarian regimes are fiendish and cruel,
and the democratic societies of the West offer a framework
for more productive lives. But this is not philosophy.
This is the wisdom of an overbearing relative, a newspaper
counseling readers on matters of social etiquette.
Perhaps you should undertake such a column yourself—
"Advice from Uncle Popper." You might begin by explaining
how to live a moral life in the shadow of atomic annihilation
amidst the putrefying civilization of the English.
It might be possible to consider the twentieth century as defined
by class struggle and Oedipal crises, as you believe,
if Marx and Freud were other than social theorists,
or worse—dogmatic quacks. Someday the ruins of Europe
will be sifted for articles of value by its conquerors

and one can only hope the last of your collected works
will have kindled a fire in some bogland long before.
After the slaughter at Cannae, Hannibal had the battlefield
searched for the bodies of the two fallen Consuls,
his own soldiers knee-deep in the blood of massacred Romans,
to demonstrate appropriate respect for a valiant foe.
Be assured I make no comparable effort on your behalf.
Language is a maze of footpaths through a quagmire
and my task is to erect signposts at dangerous junctions.
Please feel free to revisit Cambridge, Herr Professor Doktor,
but do recall that merely brandishing a fire poker
fails to express the full vigor with which I oppose your ideas.
One could make a fine crown of that poker, and I stand ready
to enact your coronation. Cordially, L. Wittgenstein

Simone de Beauvoir (1948)

Precisely because I was born into the most merciless
and refined bourgeois society in European history,
enslaved to the hierarchies of the Catholic Church
as well as the recondite social codes and pretensions
of a provincial elite desperate to differentiate itself
from the unwashed masses, desperate to preserve
the patriarchal entitlements accruing to such position—
thus am I able to speak on the subjugation of women.

Precisely because of my long relationship with Sartre,
which even I am able to recognize as an admixture
of cerebral fellowship and self-punishing debasement,
Sartre with his inexhaustible cowardice and infidelities,
all of which I have tolerated, covered up, and forgiven
on account of his intellectual gifts and my own insecurities—
thus am I able to speak about the abjection of women.

Precisely because of my wide experience in a world
from which we have been excluded, my restless travels
in America, Brazil, Africa, China, the Soviet Union,
my conversations with philosophers, housewives, luminaries—
Mao and Picasso, Rita Hayworth and Che Guevara—
my life in Paris, my life in Chicago with Algren,
because of the pyramids of Uxmal and Algerian dust
and trade unionists and café habitués and Marxist students,
because of my grasp of the sociopolitical complexity
of our plight, our servitude, our peonage, our oppression,
the one-handed grasp of men upon every lever of power,
thus am I able to speak for the liberation of women.

Precisely because we have been refused the historical right
to express our true selves, to communicate uncensored
about women's lives and experiences, about motherhood,
about otherness, distortion, male privilege, the burden
of femininity, marginalization, menstruation, sexuality,
desire that extends beyond the bedroom to the workplace
and the Panthéon, ambition fully equal to male ambition,
precisely because we have been collectively silenced
while I have fought for and won this right to expression
I am able to speak on behalf of women. So I will speak.

Mao: On History (1949)

History and the truth are like husband and wife
whose accounts of what they have witnessed
compose irreconcilable narratives.
If the Nationalists had won
we no doubt would be portrayed
as insignificant rebels, reckless insurrectionists
crushed beneath the boot heel of Chiang Kai-shek.
But the Nationalist soldiers were conscripts
dragged from their villages who deserted at the first opportunity,
while ours are bound with bonds of class devotion.

With millet and rifles we have defeated an enemy
armed with all the weapons of the West
because the will of the people is a force beyond reckoning.

Tonight, as we celebrate the victory of the People's Liberation Army,
we ride a storm of fireworks, drums and gongs
across Tiananmen Square, a great wind
sweeping from the west, the north, the east and the south.
Yet destruction of the old order is not enough.
We must establish a new society on principles
of empowerment for the masses,
we cannot waver in our commitment, twisting and swaying
like a farmer performing the rice-planting dance.
Our soldiers and our cadres must resist
the sugarcoated bullets of bourgeois entitlement.

Much is written about the productivity of capital,
as if it were a beast of legendary strength,
but Capitalism is nothing but a strong-willed pig
that has come to believe itself a dragon.

Having devoured every scrap in the pigsty
it climbs to the farmer's rooftop,
flaps its imaginary wings and leaps unto its doom.

Charlie Parker (1950)

Bird is building a metropolis with his horn.
Here are the gates of Babylon, the walls of Jericho cast down.
Might die in Chicago, Kansas City's where I was born.

Snowflake in a blizzard, purple rose before the thorn.
Stone by stone, note by note, atom by atom, noun by noun,
Bird is building a metropolis with his horn.

Uptown, downtown, following the river to its source,
Savoy, Three Deuces, Cotton Club, Lenox Lounge.
Might just die in Harlem, Kansas City's where I was born.

Bird is an abacus of possibility, Bird is riding the horse
of habit and augmented sevenths. King without a crown,
Bird is building a metropolis with his horn.

Bred to the labor of it, built to claw an eye from the storm,
made for the lowdown, the countdown, the breakdown.
Might die in Los Angeles, Kansas City's where I was born.

Bridge by bridge, solo by solo, set by set, chord by chord,
woodshed to penthouse, blue to black to brown,
Charlie Parker is building a metropolis with his horn.
Might just die in Birdland, Kansas City's where I was born.

Matisse: Vence (1951)

All my life I have lain with insomnia as with an unhappy bride
unleashing night terrors, the cries
of mythological demons kindled from inconsolable wells.
It remains a wonder each morning to discover my studio intact,
      familiar jars of brushes, my songbirds, my scissors.
Now, like a man with two wives, pain has become my constant
      companion,
pain, that old Dutch Master—
                              such meticulous particularity,
each moment hand-tinted with brown and indigo inks.

Unable to hold a brush, I sit in my wheelchair cutting paper
into ambient shapes—
swallows, coral, leaves of the philodendron.

Each age has its beauty, but this is no work for the young.

Picasso has been visiting, to relive the past and steal my ideas and
      show off his charming mistress,
and while perusing the new catalogs from America
he wondered aloud what Rothko and Motherwell and Jackson Pollock
have incorporated of our work, and who will hold us in mind when
      we are gone,
as we for so long have carried Cézanne, Renoir, Manet?

Not our rivals or critics,
not our former models or bitter wives.

The only time I met Madame Cézanne she told me that he was an
      old fool
who understood nothing about art and painted like a carpenter

crafting chairs with three unequal legs.

Not a bad analogy.

Vision is nothing if not a balancing act.

What an intense and changeable life colors live in different lights,
    as Bonnard once said.

Is he still alive?

He used to write me often, but now they are mostly dead,

disgraced during the war, or forgotten by everyone.

Posterity, let us hope, is overrated.

Crafty as ever, Pablo will outlive me, yet who can say that either of
    us shall survive to influence future generations?

Who would dare predict that any work of art will last,

that anything touched by the hand of man will live beyond the
    stench of this murderous, mirror-painted century of pain?

Mike: Hydrogen Bomb Test (1952)

mike
x-ray x-ray x-ray
moth dog sugar moth dog sugar
diablo diablo diablo diablo diablo diablo
whitney grable whitney grable whitney grable
wheeler easy john yoke huron able dormouse yeso wahoo
magnolia magnolia magnolia magnolia magnolia magnolia
starfish prime starfish prime starfish prime starfish prime starfish prime
cactus yellowwood frigate bird mohawk franklin priscilla union kepler
oak juniper fig quince tobacco rose oak juniper fig quince tobacco rose
umbrella umbrella umbrella umbrella umbrella umbrella umbrella
tumbler-snapper buster-jangle tumbler-snapper buster-jangle
vesta oberon rushmore evans wigwam plumbbob hardtack redwing
fishbowl sunbeam tightrope fishbowl sunbeam tightrope
anvil antler shrew boomer mink fisher gnome mad ringtail
armadillo armadillo armadillo armadillo armadillo
danny boy hudson ermine hognose
dead
nectar
how how how how
eel
white
black
marshmallow
haymaker climax checkmate

Frida Kahlo: Self-Portrait with Death Mask and Amputated Limb (1953)

my owl my awfulness my Aztec mask
my plaster casts my mummery my idolatrous army
my bandages my blackbird wings my needle and thread
my orb weaver my spider monkey my widow's web
my veins my serum my hopelessness my sorrows
my homicide begged and suicide borrowed
my formaldehyde my morpho butterflies my museum pieces
my necklaces my décolletage my umbilicus my sex
my power and my fruitfulness my useless caresses
my shorn hair my despair my convalescence
my still life my gangrenous dreams my stump my spine
my calvary my reaper my shock of corn
my crown of thorns my laurel wreath my curse
my mirror-muse my noose my bloodthirsty nurse

Akira Kurosawa: *Seven Samurai* (1954)

Now rain. Now chrysanthemums. Now the barley harvest.

Now mud as if the feudal age will never end.

Now hoofbeats, dust in calibrated shafts of stable light,
dragonflies above the stream, the mill wheel turning
and turning as if the feudal age will never end.

Ink, blood, smoke, rice seedlings, always the wind

and the forest which would consume it all—
village and field and social order,
devotion to illusions for which one need never apologize.

Sanctity, honor, the sublime.
                    Once more we survive.

Picasso & Françoise Gilot (1955)

Picasso

Why is the world so strangely literal, why are people so
    simpleminded in their desire for consistency?
If I say one thing now, and later another, it may be mere whim or an
    erosion of long-held belief—it is not a lie
unless I wish to deceive, and even then I often tell lies merely to add
    color to a boring conversation.

In the arena of color I have long admitted my inferiority to Matisse,
    news of whose death has reached me today.
He was the master of emerald and viridian, while I dabble pigment
    on canvas as a chef adds salt to shellfish soup.
Yet it is no lie to say I am the greatest matador in the world, even if
    the one bull I never vanquished bears Matisse's name.

In my art I am not only a hero but a god, yet in my life neither; I do
    not deny my failings, though fate has played its tricks upon me.
With Eva, perhaps, I might have remained content forever, and all
    the endless difficulties with women that followed,
their needs and jealousy, their mewling infants, everything I have
    sacrificed to wives and lovers might have been salvaged.

That was my chance, turning thirty in Montparnasse, solvent and
    unassailable—then the war began its parade of death,
my father and Apollinaire gone, the good dog, Frika, beautiful Eva
    taken by cancer, even Cubism fell to the epidemic.
No, I did not triumph over Matisse, nor was I defeated: I avoided the
    corrida that afternoon, staying home to draw doves and whores.

Françoise

Inevitably I question if I was a fool
to have given him what I did,
unconditional love and devotion
expecting nothing in return.

No—I was headstrong and drunk
on liberty as only the young can be,
before Claude and Paloma
and all that transpired between us.

It was enough, at first, to feel free,
to be with Pablo and support his work
and live within its aura, enabling
and participating in greatness.

But for Pablo love was a role to play,
like a spoiled toddler trying on attitudes,
a mask he soon tired of
and threw down in selfish outrage.

He would not harm an animal
but he would gouge a person with words
and think nothing of it,
as with Olga and Dora Maar,

as with Chagall in Saint-Jean-Cap-Ferrat,
destroying a friendship
of thirty years over lunch on a whim.
Pablo will die a child, his soul

untouched by true feeling.
You were a Venus when I met you,

he said to me, at the end.
Now you are a Christ.

No—I am a somnambulist
seeking to escape
the clutches of a despotic dream.
If cruelty is a prerequisite for immortality

then perhaps Pablo will live forever,
as he so violently desires.
If waking up brings freedom,
I am free.

Mao: On Freedom (1956)

Struggle is eternal, peace ephemeral, and conflict
the necessary means of resolving dialectical contradictions.
Therefore dissent is essential, and so I
have said to the people
let one hundred opinions contend,
let one hundred flowers bloom.

Of course, students eagerly seize such opportunity
to debate and contest their opinions,
forming political groups with romantic names
like *Bitter Medicine, Wild Grass, Spring Thunder,*
affixing wall posters and launching oratorical attacks upon the Party
for practicing "feudal socialism"
in an "arbitrary and tyrannical" fashion.
Well do I remember the enthusiasms of youth
and the danger they pose to the state.

So much has been sacrificed for the People's Republic.
I myself have lost two wives and two brothers,
Xiao Mao and his sisters, even my grown son, Anying,
killed by the American Imperialists in Korea.
Thus, untethered from human attachment,
I am like a shepherd
watching over his flock at all hours.

In the absence of warfare there is little but sex
to occupy my nights
in the Study of Chrysanthemum Fragrance
with girls selected for beauty and Party credentials
from the Cultural Work Troupes or the Bureau of Confidential Matters,
sometimes three at once in my oversized bed.

It is dangerous to accord too much power to any individual,
and were it not for my own inviolability
I would fear for China, as under Emperors of the past.

Old age is a tireless foe, but my fame as commander
is based on guile and patience—
draw the enemy in deep, then counterattack.

If instead of fragrant blossoms
the people confront us with poisonous weeds
what choice have we but to chop them down?

Elvis Presley (1957)

Here comes the train, Elvis is thinking, that must be the train
I been waiting on, coming out of the darkness now
swirling like floodwaters around him, out of the darkness
and over the muddy river, down from the hills, out and down
and over the river, cast from shadows, wrung from the ink of it,
rolling all night through Mississippi, through Tennessee,
cross those hills and along the creeks and silent valleys,
past sweat-collared towns on soft-paved roads
with the crossing light flashing, past cotton fields and carpet mills
and hog pens and dented corncribs, clatter and rattle
coming down the line, coming round the bend,
echo and reverb in the hollow body of that torn-raw country,

Elvis is tapping his fingers restlessly, alone in the moonlight
on the darkened platform, Elvis is never alone,
where's the Colonel, he wonders, where's the fellas tonight,

Elvis is eating a hamburger at Chenault's Drive-In,
Elvis is eating mashed potatoes and brown gravy
and fried chicken and his mama's special coconut cake,

Elvis is shopping for clothes at Lansky's with all the sharp dressers,
the Colored folks who have an eye for that stuff,
an eye and an ear and a style Elvis honors and amplifies,

Elvis is driving all night to the next gig with Bill and Scotty,
the next roadhouse or Elks club or high school auditorium,
stopping the car to buy firecrackers at every stand they pass,
Elvis is headed to Shreveport, Omaha, Jacksonville, Houston,
Elvis is headed to Iuka, Mississippi, and Leechville, Arkansas,

and all the little towns and cities scattered across Texas,

Roy Orbison catches the show in Odessa,
Buddy Holly in Lubbock,

Elvis is onstage snarling and yelping and fucking with them,
strutting, tomcatting, spitting his gum into the audience,
Elvis is acting the fool, the bad boy, a punk in a kelly green suit
and the shoes of a divorce court lawyer
and the hair of a truck driver and the voice of a hillbilly
and the swivel of a Beale Street bluesman,
surly and longing and swaggering and joyous
as if to erase the centuries of dust and brute labor,
as if to eviscerate his people's long history of desperation
and Depression and war and impoverishment,

though not of the soul, surely, for he loves Jesus as a brother,

like a fire, that spirit, like a candle, that devotion,
that desire, that honey-coated tongue of longing,

what does he want, what does he want

popping handfuls of sleeping pills at the Sahara,
blacking out the windows with tinfoil and masking tape,
what is he hungering for if not the rhinestone glitter
of the cat's-eye in the ice cubes spilled in red dirt,
searching everywhere for that sparkle and shine,
for the quicksilver he's been chasing since he first felt it
walking the streets of Memphis at night so long ago,
singing spirituals in church, driving his motorcycle
fast and reckless with a girl's arms around him,
June and Dixie and Anita and Priscilla,

searching for something he has never been able to name,
even in the only language he has ever spoken with fluency,
music, the upsurge of song, the seizure and release of it,

searching for beauty in a world of tarnish and obligation,
a world of homespun dresses and Formica countertops,
searching in Tupelo, in Beverly Hills, in the cold Kentucky rain,

Elvis is courteous and deferential and patriotic,
Elvis is posing for publicity stills, gracious and patient,
Elvis is a natural, Elvis is eager to please,
Elvis is eating crowder peas and burnt-crisp bacon,
Elvis is in three movies a year, real Hollywood movies,
Elvis is a gunslinger and Elvis is a race-car driver
a pilot a photographer a soldier a tuna fisherman,
Elvis can hardly bear to sing the songs
for the sound track album, man, this shit is awful,
Elvis is water-skiing, playing touch football,
Elvis is renting out the Rainbow Rollerdrome for his cronies,
Elvis is pranking everyone at the studio with a joy buzzer,
even the head of RCA Records, the Colonel
nods his disapproval, not the place or time for it, son,

the Colonel with his percentages and dimestore stogies,

Elvis is watching the yellow vinyl 78s emerge from the press
at Buster Williams Plastic Products on Chelsea Avenue,
"That's All Right b/w Blue Moon of Kentucky,"

you can't knock success, now, I'm just thankful to the fans,
thankful my mama and daddy brought me up right,
thankful I could rise above the trials and circumstances,

Elvis is eating it up, Elvis is having a ball, Elvis is dying
to escape the little house on Lamar Avenue
with his daddy fixing the car on the lawn out front,

to escape his mama with her peanut butter and banana sandwiches
and her pains and her never-ending worry for her boy,
Lord knows how much he loved her
but the world is bursting into flames now, Mama,
the world is igniting with all the glory of teenage desire,

as if his heart was on fire with it, burning up with it,
shouting and bellowing, praising and inciting it,
throwing gasoline onto his own funeral pyre,

as if fame were an act of self-immolation,

the world is opening the throttle and rattling down the rails
because there has to be somewhere to get to,
he can feel it in the balls of his feet,
in the stutter and dip of knee and hip, he can see it
and hear it there, across the street, across the river,
coming round the bend, coming down the line,

Elvis loved his mama but the Lord called her to Him,

SHE WAS THE SUNSHINE OF OUR HOME

they engraved on her tombstone and it was the truth,
Elvis loved his mama even when she understood
that her boy was changing and slipping away,
that she was losing him to the lure of show business,

maybe you ought to come back to Memphis and drive the truck
for the electric company again, son, despite all the money,

how the Colonel would chortle at that, well now,
the Colonel with all his machinations and glib charm,
that's a lot of money to turn your back on, Mizz Gladys,
maybe we better ask Elvis what he makes of all this,

now Mama, there's nothing wrong with being famous,
everybody wants to be famous, that's just how it is,

but already the girls are scrawling their numbers in lipstick
on the side of the Cadillac wherever he parks it,
already they wait day and night outside the gates
for an autograph, for a wave, for a glimpse,
and it is not quite natural, she sees, their desire
to touch and to worship him, her darling boy,
to wipe the sweat from his brow and tear his clothing to tatters,
to rend, to salve, to proclaim, to glorify,

fetishism is not a word in her vocabulary, why should it be,

how could she know, how could any of them imagine
that America would feast upon his body,
devour him like wasps consuming a rotten pear,

there is no rock and roll until he ennobles it,
there is no Baby Boom until he enables it,
there is no cultural commodification until he embodies it,
there is no cult of celebrity until he enacts it,

Elvis is kissing Natalie Wood, kissing Ann-Margret,
Elvis is on *The Ed Sullivan Show* watched by 82 percent of the US of A,
Elvis is tossing his ruby-jeweled eagle cape into the crowd,
Elvis is demonstrating karate moves at the studio in Nashville,
tape is rolling and the band is getting restless, they haven't cut a
    single song,

Elvis is a prisoner of the merchandise and syringes,
the gold sequins and white leather furniture,
Elvis is nodding off at the table, falling asleep
with scrambled eggs slipping down his face,
one of the boys rushes over to fix him up,
Elvis is staring into the yard behind Graceland
at the motorcycles and chicken coop and the pillars
around the swimming pool shining in the moonlight,

Mama won't be feeding them chickens no more, son,
his daddy told him, the day they laid her in the grave,
Mama won't be feeding them chickens no more,

Elvis is riding through his mother's tulip bed
on the lawnmower just for a lark, how she hollered at him,
hollered and then laughed, everybody laughing,
they'd just moved into Graceland, he bought it for her,

Elvis is crying, Elvis is swallowing pills by the dozen—
Demerol and Placidyl, codeine and Dilaudid—
but the pain won't go away, the sorrow and confusion
and the sound of the train coming closer,

everything is clouds and fog and darkness on the platform,
silver light against swirling shadows, like a movie screen,
Elvis loves the pictures, loves the velvet mythos of it,

maybe this is just a movie, everything is just a movie,
maybe it's not a train but the sound of wasps,
Elvis is thinking, maybe it's them wasps coming for me,

Elvis is alone on the platform but Elvis is never alone,
Elvis is on the bathroom floor, golden pajamas
around his ankles, rug soaked with vomit,

Elvis is a mountain, Elvis is a rainstorm,
Elvis is a rose in a pool of muddy Mississippi River water,

something is coming, he can't remember what,
a train or a tiger or an angel with a trumpet,
something is coming and he can see it now,

the train is coming into the station and Elvis is getting on,
what fool wouldn't, what fool wouldn't
grasp the whistle and gospel of that mystery,

and as the train begins to move Elvis remembers
so many things he'd forgotten—the feeling
of wind in his hair, the sound of oak leaves at midnight,

the train is pulling out, the train is leaving Memphis
and Elvis is on board, he might be waving
as they come to the first bend, and then the train is gone.

Mao: On the Great Leap Forward (1958)

When I announce my intention to swim in Three Great Rivers
my secretaries and advisors react with outrage.
The water is too dirty, they protest, and there is danger
from currents, and mud holes, and whirlpools.
What in this world is pure? I ask them.
What in this world is free of risk?
So I swam two hours in the Pearl River
amidst the mud and sewage of the countryside
and they had no choice but to flounder alongside me,
leaping from the boat fully dressed,
some of them unable to swim at all, the fools.

If a tiger never brushes its teeth why should I?

I rinse my mouth with green tea before bed,
as I was taught as a child,
as good peasants still do in southern provinces.
If my teeth blacken and rot, so be it. I have endured
far worse in service to the Revolution.

I fear for the future of the People's Republic.
The Party has grown conservative, inelastic.
Marx, I have come to fear, is like a new Confucius,
and the party leaders move like slaves
to his dogma with no drive or imagination.
It is time to stir up the sediment,
to set the people against the Party itself.
Snow lasts longest in the shadows of great peaks.
Jiang Qing has six toes.
I occupy myself with dance parties
and reading Chinese history in my bathrobe at poolside.

When I swim in the ocean at Beidaihe
the security men try to frighten me
with accounts of shark attacks.

Imagine a peasant too fastidious
to muck the shit from his stables.
Imagine the husband of a six-toed woman
worried about swimming with sharks.

Willem de Kooning (1959)

And now I sit in state, a museum piece enthroned,
a statue of the Triumphant Individual alone
with my orb and scepter, my pocket flask, my corona of motes,
alone with my famous brushstroke, that black voluptuary,
that phantasm, that old philandering psychopomp,
that Netherlandish crony whispering *long live the king.*
And now, crowned to rule unrivaled,
I feel nothing but nostalgia for the way it was
in the summer of '54 at the Red House in Bridgehampton,
Franz and Jackson still alive, the whole gang,
the parties, girls and booze, painting
in the imperial manner all night in the garage,
famous, almost famous, heroic, still poor,
still poor but nearly famous, on the cusp, at the threshold,
poor so long we could imagine no real use for money
and still wanting it and already aware that it,
all of it—fame and wealth, *Time* and *Life*—
would pose a problem in perspective
we would never really solve,
an eternally receding *trompe l'oeil*
of dealers and day-trippers and glad-handers,
weeklong binges in the darkest dead-end Bowery bars,
all that against the way we had been, like soldiers
near the end of the war—and what a war—
whose wounds would never heal for all that we bathed them
daily in Scotch whisky.
After years of diligent squinting at last
I began to see the light
within darkness, to stow my baggage
on untempered canvas—fear, sorrow, exile, lust—
as years ago, a stowaway bearing the moniker of a king,

a Dutchman bound for Manhattan four hundred years too late,
I hid in the boiler room and watched a new world
fill the frame of the porthole with its arrogance
and brute logic, its discipline of chaos,
a firestorm into which I would unhesitatingly throw myself
once more feeling nothing
but gratitude for the chance to burn.

BOOK FOUR

Zora Neale Hurston: Enigmatic Atlas (1960)

Zora: z to $a;$ a name, an anagram, an enigmatic atlas.

Youth, sweet and spurious as a pirate's treasure map,
x marks the spot, X for Christ arisen in Eatonville,
wandering tribes of the Niger, the Congo, the Zambezi,
voodoo children unshackled but still bound to that cross.

Under the great green hands of the chinaberry trees
tribulations shadowed my girlhood, but I
sought always the light of knowledge, sought
release from the strictures of social circumstance,
queen of my own empowered imagination.

Poverty rots the soul, powerlessness unmans us.
Only in Harlem could I spar with equals,
New York an apple of which I bit, and swallowed.

My wings were ever the mockingbird's, my eyes
loved mirrors, my pen drew ink from an echoing well,
kin-pool, deep reservoir of African blood.

Just as I learned to smile for white folks in Memphis
I mastered the anthropologist's dialect at Columbia,
hoodoo lingo of the academic idiolect,
glorification of folklore into ethnographic gospel. O, but

Florida, I could never escape your prodigal soil.

Eau Gallie, my final home, a garden for gourds,
despair, and forgetfulness, my memory and my works

consigned to the oblivion of a debtor's bonfire
because I chose to speak my people's truth unaltered,
and so lay claim to all history's sorrows.

Jane Goodall (1961)

Our century, our life and times, will be remembered
not for its artistic glory or triumphs of technology
but for its incalculable losses, for rain-matted bodies
at makeshift markets on the road to Kisangani,
civets, dik-diks, monkeys, anteaters, elephants, apes,
dead animals, vanished species, the earth's ravishment
by humankind, our kind, by you and by me.
Even as we recoil at the thought of ancient savagery,
cannibalism in some tribal past, medieval tortures,
our great-great-grandparents' embrace of slavery,
so the future will hold us accountable for this holocaust
against our brothers and sisters. What makes us human
makes us fellow creatures, creeping things,
fauna of a fragile terrestrial biosphere,
neither more nor less. All lives are consequential,
there is no hierarchy of consciousness or intellect.
To feel the warm, oxygenated exhalation of the jungle
is to know life as the planet intended it,
morning fog above the forest is the earth's imagination
made literal, hovering and nourishing. Great trees
are more humble and profound than we could ever be,
as I learned my first lonely year at Gombe.
Who can say why Africa had been my lifelong dream,
but it was and when the chance arose I seized it,
settled in Nairobi, adopted a mongoose, two bush babies,
a vervet monkey and a prickly hedgehog named Dinkie.
When I met Louis Leakey at the museum I scarcely believed
my good fortune to be invited to accompany his family
on their annual archaeological dig at Olduvai Gorge.
What makes us human abides in the red earth
of Olduvai. That was my first sight of the Serengeti

with its sun-gold grasslands and copses of thorn trees
and soda water lakes full of raucous flamingos
where I would later spend years with my son and husband
studying wild dogs and hyenas and Egyptian vultures
amidst herds of antelope and eland, zebras and wildebeest,
ponds full of hippos, solitary rhinos, the cheetah
who strode elegantly beside our Land Rover that first day
when everything was new and wonderful,
even the toil of the dig, that meticulous detective work,
sifting and searching for the one, improbable shard
or fragment of skull or jawbone amidst the uncountable
chips, sherds, lithic flakes, lacework bones of mice,
fossilized tusks of long-extinct elephant species,
baboon teeth so like our own, rock, stone, soil,
archival crypt of the upright walkers, the long of shank,
the clever ones who left the protection of the forest
for the abundant plains, hunters on the savanna,
Homo habilis, Homo erectus, Homo sapiens. What makes us
human mimicks the teardrop shape of the hand
in the hand ax knapped from flint a million years ago.
What makes us human makes us need to know
what makes us human. At night I would drag my cot
to sleep blanketed by wind amidst those vast plains
beneath the mysterious mirroring immenseness of the Milky Way.
Sweet and ineffectual lecher that he was, Louis
prowled sniffing around our tents like a golden jackal
but he meant no harm, he was lonely and Mary
was a scold and a drinker, I pitied them both.
One evening, Gillian and I took the dalmatians for a walk
after dinner and were perhaps a mile from camp
when a thrill shivered my spine and a voice in my head
said clearly *there is a lion beneath the acacia tree*
before my eyes had begun to unpuzzle his shadow
and then he stood, a young male, curious at the sight of us.

Gillian wanted to hide which of course was all wrong.
Talking cheerfully, I led us slowly up the gorge,
keeping in plain sight, and soon enough he turned aside
and disappeared into the brush. Three years later,
thanks to Louis's tireless work and charm and vision,
I arrived at Gombe accompanied—since the authorities
refused to permit a white woman alone in the wild—
by my indomitable English mother, Vanne.
Looking back to the beauty of Lake Tanganyika
in those years, the fisherman's huts, forested valleys
below the steep eroded cliffs of the escarpment,
buffalo paths through grass ten feet tall,
sanctity of the jungle that ran across the hills
from Tanzania to Uganda to Rwanda to the Congo,
before logging roads, before machine guns and helicopters,
before wars of greed and territorialism and extermination,
wars both ape and human, looking back
from the crumbling precipice of the present day
it seems simple to recognize nature's devastating helplessness
in the face of our advantages—not strength or courage
but technology and ruthlessness and sheer numbers.
When I think of myself then, I must struggle to unlearn
everything I know about the chimps, sink backward
past all the documented births, deaths, discoveries,
to recall first contacts, first instances,
the first encounters in which they came to accept or,
at least, refrained from flight at the sight of me,
those months when I saw only jungle and desired
nothing more in my eagerness than a glimpse
of a black arm reaching out from thick foliage
to grasp the fruit of the *msulula* tree.
It was David Greybeard who tolerated me, unafraid,
as I hunched and waited, equally curious,
creature to creature, across a clearing in the jungle.

Even then it was obvious that what he expressed
was not "behavior" but sentience, deep and purposeful
intelligence—any clear-eyed, open-minded observer
would recognize at once our startling similarity,
just the way he sat and watched me watching him,
one knee bent, one arm scratching his back,
the other hand stroking his beard, thumb across top lip,
like some Victorian ship captain or eccentric uncle.
To call these familiar gestures "human-like"
misses everything—they are "chimp-like" gestures,
they belong to us equally, a shared inheritance.
Chimps are our veiled reflection in time's mirror,
rough drafts, pots drawn early from the kiln.
In a universe of vast unlikeness, a universe
of voids and atoms and protozoa, we are first cousins,
next of kin. What makes us human makes us
forked branches on evolution's zygotic tree.
Of course giving them names was wrong—Flo and Fifi,
Goblin and David Greybeard and Mr. McGregor—
sentimental, anthropomorphic, unscientific,
but isn't that what we do, name the world, create order
in our heart's image? As surely they gave to me
a name composed of odor, posture, uncouth movements,
my skin of repetitive khaki cloth, my long pale hair,
a name composed of habits, and habitation,
She Who Lives in the Strange Hard Nest,
She of the Bananas and Eggs, She Who Swims,
She Who Watches from the Peak, who sees our life
in the forest as it has been for millions of years,
who bears witness to the abyss of its annihilation,
she who comes to write our epitaph, or to save us.

The Pulse of the Planet (1962)

> The steady accumulation of facts—cold, dry and objective, one
> piled upon the other in endless succession—finally produces a
> vivid and frightening image of a dynamic and dangerous planet.
>
> *—THE PULSE OF THE PLANET: A REPORT*
> *FROM THE SMITHSONIAN INSTITUTION CENTER*
> *FOR SHORT-LIVED PHENOMENA*

Millions of leaf-cutting ants devastate tea and cocoa crops in
 southern Peru.
Swarms of field mice imperil the Australian grain harvest.
The kouprey, a species of Cambodian forest ox, is reported on the
 verge of extinction.

A coal-mine explosion kills 299 in Saarland, West Germany.
Flash floods kill 440 in Barcelona.
4,000 die in an avalanche in Nevado Huascarán, Peru.

John Glenn orbits the earth three times in *Friendship 7.*
Telstar, the first commercial communications satellite, is launched.
Ranger 4 spacecraft malfunctions and crashes into the moon.

James Meredith becomes the first black student at the University of
 Mississippi.
Wilt Chamberlain scores one hundred points in an NBA game.
Jimi Hendrix is honorably discharged from the US Army due to
 "lack of interest."

The Beatles audition unsuccessfully for Decca Records.
Bob Dylan's self-titled debut album is released by Columbia Records.
Axl Rose is born.

William Faulkner dies, Herman Hesse dies, e. e. cummings dies.
Rachel Carson's *Silent Spring* launches American environmental
    movement.
The Incredible Hulk #1 is published by Marvel Comics.

Nelson Mandela is arrested in South Africa for "incitement to
    rebellion."
Charles de Gaulle recognizes Algerian independence from France.
Adolf Eichmann is executed in Israel.

In Southern California, the first Taco Bell opens in Downey,
Marilyn Monroe overdoses on sleeping pills in Brentwood,
Andy Warhol premieres *32 Campbell's Soup Cans* at the Ferus Gallery.

A fire begun at the town dump spreads into abandoned mines
and coal seams below Centralia, Pennsylvania;
it will burn for the rest of the century.

The first Kmart opens in Garden City, Michigan,
the first Target in Roseville, Minnesota,
and the first Wal-Mart in Rogers, Arkansas.

I am born.

Sylvia and Ted (1963)

Upon reading a biography of Ted Hughes given to me
by Kerry Hardie in Dublin

They say you cannot pin the tale of her sorrow to his donkey,
cannot disengage her Cleopatra from his asp,
that we must disregard the sound of her typing up his stories
in the cold Boston winter of 1958, glossy recipes
clipped from magazines for sophisticated young ladies
to appease her father's ghost and her marvelous man.

Alas, life and works disintegrate alike when Sylvia departs,
absent her ardor the biography slogs and equivocates
to rationalize the prerogatives of a British gentleman,

after all it is 1967
and we are very modern, it is 1970

and his amorous peregrinations seem incommensurate
with even the most cursory code of interpersonal ethics,
tragedy rendered absurd by a cloak
of narcissistic mysticism and astrological predestination,

the maraudings of an unencumbered masculine ego
like an ambulatory Ogham stone rampaging across the moors
leaving a trail of crushed geese, mangled hedgehogs
and farmers' daughters ravished in its wake.

But in those first bitter, frost-glittered weeks of 1963
Sylvia wanders alone the unharvested fields
of her imagination, her mind in the days before death
a small engine jammed open full-throttle,

smell of gas and the smoking volts of the electroshock ward
and the words in their cascade within her, waterfall
of liquid metals, each poem a pail dipped into that flow,
dark maw, paltry and inadequate, it spills
but it holds.

And there, across the elemental river, stands Ted,
predatory, crag-browed, boreal, druidic,
digging with loy and mattock an open grave
beneath the mortuary elm in which to bury himself
on the morning of her suicide and every dawn thereafter
alongside his feral familiars—hawk, stoat, pike.

Ted and Sylvia. Sylvia and Ted.

Let us remember them by their claw marks.

The Coltrane Changes (1964)

John Coltrane is flying
further into the darkness
trying to learn why it sings,
why it sparkles and hearkens

at the plunge of a valve,
at the throb of a string,
Coltrane is trying
to learn everything, to solve

for the enharmonic unknown
within his own heart,
hurtling toward sainthood
scarred and enlightened and bent

at every joint, every staff or bar
he's ever been wounded by,
called by the dark star
of art to witness, and testify.

The Style for Dylan (1965)

Adorable Bob, deplorable Bob, not yet mascara-and-fedora Bob, lean
and hungry, all cheekbones, fawn and leopard skin,
ain't got nothing to lose Bob, adrenaline and Benzedrine Bob,
hungry and frugal, positively 4th and MacDougal Street Bob,
wings of Mercury Bob, hermetic and copacetic Bob, poetic Bob in his
pointed shoes and bells, glibly Shakespearean,
high-toned and empyrean, rollicking, frolicsome Bob hitting only
high notes, prime-time Bob wraithlike in the limelight,
swanning, sneering, bejeweled in black shades, baby-faced Bob with a
headful of snakes, meal-scrounging changeling chasing the dragon,
O precious gifted snarling unrefusable Parnassian haughty habit-
forming Bob, masterful and disaster prone, wicked and aquiline,
working-stiff Bob, put you on the day shift Bob, swaggering and
stomping in the back alley Bob, folkways Bob, payday Bob, next-
in-line-for-the-big-time Bob,
strung-out Bob, everybody-who-was-hanging-out Bob, cast down
and resurrected, chooga-looga bluesman manqué,
rock-and-roll Bob lifting the riff from "La Bamba," stealing a march
on Lennon & McCartney, revolutionary youth to the electrified
barricades,
plugged-in Bob, Stratocaster Bob kicking out the jams, fortune and
fame Bob, bridge and chorus, verse and refrain Bob,
Bob the troubadour caught in a revolving door, crowned with
laurels, crowned with thorns, amphetamine Bob cruising the
skyline in a Buick 6,
hansom cab and Detroit chariot Bob, Triumph motorcycle and freight
train Bob, bootstrap Bob, imposter Bob, Judas Iscariot Bob,
ear to the ground Bob and burn it down Bob, hey you get off of my
cloud Bob, whatever you do, play it fuckin' loud, Bob.

Andy Warhol: Image, Print, Negative (1966)

egg.

imprimatur.

apparent. ego. ink.

message. sphinx. negation.

magus. pun. tint. scrimp. scrimmage.

agate. imprints. pregnant. impish. nascent.

homage. wedge. limn. lint. tent. tenth. tentative.

pruny. impugn. vegetative. inflate. hymn. ant. bridge. runt.

tithe. begat. pejorative. rant. writhed. rental. retail. contrapuntal.

iamb. imbed. nag. got. tiff. obdurate. illustrative. sacrilege.

engage. gouge. magic. pint. punt. maculate. gateaux.

plangent. agency. tango. mandible. unabridged.

skinflint. imago. ergo. prink. squint. trinity.

plumage. damage. slippage. spillage.

ingot. votive. mar. par. prince.

putative. imagist. vista.

emerge. negate.

map.

The Death of Edward Hopper (1967)

1.

Night after night the foghorn
like a great horned owl watching over the harbor,
boats in and out with their trawls and gigs,

rosebushes behind the town museum
with its spoked wheel from the sunken skipjack
whose mast emerges from a sand dune

like an eruptive stork leg,
and the original Fresnel lens from the lighthouse
a lapidary, many-petaled crystal flower,

swollen magnolia blossoms at twilight,
tree like a dewy, perfumed chandelier,
and the hushed grass beneath the cedars

at that hour when the sky eases toward ashes,
then darker, darker, night not a veil descending
but a hand rising up, clenching us in its palm.

2.

Not a misanthrope, not a swain of solitude,
not averse to heavy breasts
spilling from a beige silk nightgown,

not afraid of the body but more at home
with sunlight infiltrating empty rooms,
the veneer of bleached calcium on oyster shells,

freight cars, brick walls, seaside hills.
Endurance and austerity.
Ardent restraint.

Brushstrokes aloof as iridescent soap bubbles,
flocked clouds reflected in car windows,
umbrellas on city avenues like algal blooms,

the illusion of riches in a teaspoon of puddle-water
and the domestic suns of dandelions
shining everywhere, everywhere, everywhere.

3.

Carnival attractions at sunset in late summer,
Sea Dragon, Tilt-a-Whirl, The Scrambler,
disorienting blurs of candescent motion

that conclude with a staggering-forth like birth,
a reemergence, shaken and laughing,
into the popcorn-scented dusk.

You would think that was the end of it
but they come again—singly and in pairs,
strapped into little egg- and saucer-shaped cars,

defenseless in the last raw streamers of sunlight,
they wait, all starkness and vulnerability,
for the ride to start.

And the onlookers leaning against a picket fence
behold in those luminous faces
all the loneliness and longing of American life.

Picasso & Jacqueline Roque (1968)

Picasso

A canvas comprises a totality of surface
just as Spain is composed of constituent parts,
Catalunya, Madrid, hills and trees, etc.

Color dyes the fabric clothing form itself,
as wars and anthems unify
the body politic of mass and volume.

Neutral as Switzerland, the palette
confers legitimacy on every pigment it holds,
like a Roman Emperor. Zaragoza,

that dusty, lemon-bitter city of rough stones
with its cathedral of saints' bones
on a plaza lacking any compensatory grace—

Zaragoza is but the corruption
of its Roman name, Caesaraugusta,
and so a cohort to historical inaccuracy.

This I propose as demonstration
that what matters is not accuracy but acts,
not chronicles but conquests.

The body is everything I have wished
to rid myself of through art
and failed. Yet surrender is impossible.

My hands persevere in the task of painting
as soldiers long after the battle is lost
carry on their raping of women in the streets.

Jacqueline

And I shall salt his palms with my tears.
And I shall seal the tomb of his ears

against trespass and regret.
I am the last, do not forget.

And I shall never rest.
I shall nurse his scepter with my breasts,

bolt the gates of his eyes
against friends and spies.

Pigeons and orphans swirl
in my sable pelt, my tongue of pearl.

And I shall keep the tower fast.
And I shall be the last.

Apollo (1969)

This would be the vessel of our dismantling,
whose flames propose to outshine the divine
as science declares itself nemesis to myth.

What is science but a wondrous supposition
to shield yourselves from chaos, to explain,
as we once did, the order of the universe?

No, Helios's chariot does not transport the sun—
is that why you came, to steal his horses?
Is that why you voyaged to this negligible rock?

Earth, too, is a stone in a sea of darkness,
and now you are orphaned there, marooned
within your clouded atmosphere of reason.

Destroying us will not reduce your insignificance.
Selene, that beautiful dreamer, will not vanish
because you plant a banner on her orb.

Did you think the moon her residence? Fools.
She lives where all gods do, as everything
you exalt and rage against does: in you.

Jacques Derrida (1970)

The Ticking Clock (1971)

Snoop Dogg is born, Julian Assange is born. Already it is coming,
already the new century—though we have hardly begun
to imagine the death of the old—is taking shape around us.
Babies are crying in nurseries, toddlers are shaking their rattles.
A tennis star is born in Germany, a footballer in Nigeria.
Downhill skiers are born, prime ministers, business tycoons,
pop stars whose images will paper the streets of Tokyo and Bangkok.
Barack Obama is ten years old. Hillary Rodham has just begun
to date her down-home Yale Law classmate, Bill Clinton.
Vladimir Putin is a student at Leningrad State University.
Major General Idi Amin Dada seizes power in Uganda.
Century of integrated circuits & blue plastic radios,
century of self-conscious fabrication, century of human moons.
Larry Page and Sergey Brin will not be born for two more years,
information technology is a euphemism for paper and pencil.
At MIT, Ray Tomlinson decides to employ the @ sign
in the address of the very first email, which he sends
over the ARPANET to another computer in the same room:
"Don't tell anyone," he confesses to a friend,
"but this is not what we're supposed to be working on."
Uma Thurman is an infant. Princess Diana is a shy girl
in boarding school; she will not survive the century.
Tupac Shakur is born but he will not survive it.
Jim Morrison dies in a bathtub in Paris—*no one here gets out alive.*
The south tower of the World Trade Center is topped out
at 1,368 feet, officially the tallest building in the world.
In Kafr el-Sheikh, Mohammed Atta is three years old.
Coco Chanel dies. Reinhold Niebuhr, Igor Stravinsky
and Louis Armstrong die. Lance Armstrong is born.
The future is being assembled in the expanding neural webs
of six-year-olds, in the atoms of the yet-to-be-incarnated

beings we imagine as holographic ghosts sitting awkwardly
in the waiting room of the future. Adriano Moraes,
the Brazilian rodeo champion, is one; Wyclef Jean is two.
Agnes Martin will not resume painting for three more years.
The twentieth century is vanishing, o radiant century,
century of quarter notes & treble clefs, of chalk on black paper,
century of deliverance & self-deception, expediency & lies.
Duane Allman crashes his Harley, Edie Sedgwick OD's,
Dean Acheson and Gene Vincent die on the same day.
George Seferis dies. Pablo Neruda wins the Nobel Prize
but has only eighteen months to live. Bertrand Russell,
Yukio Mishima and Jimi Hendrix were buried last year.
Ogden Nash has died; no one lives forever, but he tried.
Lin Biao is dead, his coup against the aging Mao a failure.
Deng Xiaoping has been sent to the provinces for reeducation
at the Xinjian County Tractor Factory: he will reemerge.
China will follow the Capitalist road; *to be rich is glorious.*
Alan Shepard hits the very first golf ball on the moon.
Daisuke Enomoto, Japan's first space tourist, is born.
George Lucas directs his first film, Wes Anderson is two,
Kubrick releases *A Clockwork Orange*, Guillermo del Toro is seven.
Jimmy Wales attends a Montessori school in Alabama:
Wikipedia cannot be found in any glossary or reference text.
Soon there will be no need for glossaries or reference texts.
Bird is dead, Monk is crazy, Miles has turned his back,
Elvis is lost, John Lennon no longer believes in Beatles.
As Disney World opens the Manson Family are on trial
and America's largest underground nuclear test, *Cannikin*,
detonates beneath Amchitka in the Aleutian Islands.
Behold, I am alpha and omega. The world is being destroyed,
the world is being created anew; the century is dying,
the century is being born. The clock is ticking.

Mao: On the Future (1972)

Some believe that millions died of starvation
during the Great Leap Forward,
they say the peasants harvesting rice in colorful native outfits
were stage-managed along the tracks of my private train
for the purpose of misleading me.
On behalf of the Party I say they are wrong
and the Party controls the facts
as an officer commands recruits in the ranks.

What I love best are great upheavals.
Revolution begets revolution.
Time alone opposes me now, and so time
must be struggled against, reeducated, rectified.
Only the young are strong enough,
only the Red Guard will show no clemency
against ancestor tablets and ancient texts,
against temple gates, mahjong tiles, Hong Kong dresses.
Even those who keep caged songbirds
shall be denounced as subversives, reactionary agents
of a past seeking always to reestablish its dominion.

The destruction of mankind
would be a small thing in the universe.
Do not imagine that apes are the only animal
capable of advanced evolution—
I can envision a time in which pigs, or horses,
or some forest shrew evolves to occupy our position
and perhaps the world would be better for it.
So I say to our former brothers in the Soviet Union

as I have said to the West

that we would welcome a nuclear attack

for the clarity and resolve it would bestow upon us.

In my lifetime we have advanced

from rickshaws to jet engines, the abacus to electronic computations.

If we sold wheat for money to build atomic bombs

during a time of starvation I do not apologize for it.

If millions died for progress the price was not too high.

We can afford to lose far more.

Tens of millions, hundreds of millions,

such numbers are meaningless abstractions.

The future does not scruple

over census records. Who stops to count

every star in the sky

will never see the Milky Way.

You cannot eat a watermelon

without spitting out some seeds.

Picasso (1973)

1.

You ask what I truly remember of it—everything and nothing.
The cries of peacocks in the Moorish ruins of Málaga,
Ménerbes where the owls swooped down at dusk
to carry off the rib-thin village cats, a night in Naples
when Stravinsky and I were arrested for pissing in the Galleria,
Alfred Jarry's pistol, the statuettes stolen from the Louvre,
the sea, of course, the Mediterranean shining olive-silver
on a day we sailed out from the white harbor of Cadaqués
and Frika swam after us, so deep we let her clamber aboard,
soaking the skiff as she shook her glittering fur.
And *la vie Américaine* in the '20s with Gerald and Sara Murphy
and Scott Fitzgerald pouring their dollars into the sea
off the rocks in Cap d'Antibes like flat champagne,
and I supporting Olga in the style to which she aspired,
a chauffeur to guide our immense Hispano-Suiza
through the village streets of Paris, and servants and maids
and white shoes and dinner jackets and diapers and headaches
and the Dadaists and the balletomanes and the war
between Cocteau and Breton and Satie and Massine
and the dealers and the bankers and at last Marie-Thérèse
to alleviate the weight of all that money upon my soul.

2.

In human affairs everything is craven, tainted, exigent.
Only art may live beyond compromise.
But merely the intention to create is not enough.

Sometimes bronze is too luxurious, marble too intense,
pebbles shaped by the sea too masterful to equal.
The world provides a treasury from which to choose—
paper or canvas, gouache or charcoal or ink.

Even in my life there were days when the work would not come,
when the child had the measles and the wife was a shrew,
when rain on slate made we wonder how I ever felt affection for Paris.

The Mediterranean rejuvenated me,
junk rejuvenated me.

Bored, I searched the scrap heap and potter's field
for broken urns and jug handles, string and wire,
wicker baskets I might put to use in some assemblage.

Driving home through Aix after the bullfights I stopped
always at the same candy store to buy their almond-paste *calissons*,
not for the sugar but the sturdy, diamond-shaped box,
which, filled with plaster, creates an ideal base for a sculpture.

Yes, to see is to possess, and you must invest heart and soul
in the work, but not all hearts and souls are equal.
How much must be poured until a vessel runs over depends
on the size of the vessel, how much must be drunk
depends on the strength of the liquor.

For Braque, a bottle or two of good wine.
For Matisse, a glass of Armagnac.
For Picasso—a spoonful, a thimble, a single drop of blood.

3.

This afternoon, waking from siesta, I watched a column
of light slip between the wavering curtains,
certain as a bar of gold, solid as the cast-iron truss
for some incalculable architecture of the air.
Closing my eyes, the darkness was faceted and cloven
by that brilliant negative, that linear declension
imprinted upon the cornea in an infinite planar regression.

It was a vision of Cubism, I recognized at once,
an argument for its strategy of representation,
its assault upon the viewer, its fragmentation
of continuity and surface into theoretical instances.
I admire it still, but its self-consciousness exhausts me.
I feel as if the canvasses are inspecting my studio
with their insectlike eyes, studying and judging me.

Cubism was like the desert in the American cowboy movies,
or the olive-starred uplands around Horta de Ebro,
a wilderness to be crossed at any cost—
gold dust, drinking water, the lives of the animals—
everything sacrificed for a journey without destination.

Sometimes, waking like that in the heat of afternoon,
things come back to me and I feel not young
but ageless, primordial, like fresh clay in the hands.
Of course it is an illusion. The body withers, the body fades.
Only art carries on, like a riderless horse,
wandering the bone-colored desolation of the canvas.

4.

Among the many forms of human desire, the only one
I cannot claim as an intimate is the wish to surrender
to the prerogatives of a fevered abstraction,
renunciation to the posturing of saviors and overlords,
capitulation of the self to Jesus or Franco or Stalin.

If birds and the sea are not enough, if all figures erode
to sand and representation proves insufficient,
what likelihood that conceptualizations will sustain me?

Whatever they were thinking in the painted caves
it was not to submit to a regime of monotony,
not to weigh themselves down but to lighten the load
of their burdens. Even then they knew that art
was called up from a deep source to enrich human life,
not hermetic but invigorating, not ideological but erotic
as pigment palmed across bare rock and naked skin.

If the Mediterranean piles its silver treasure in my arms,
if the cooing of doves prove balm to my ears,
if the sun, if the moon, if the cock, if the she-goat—
if the world is the only idiom I have mastered
why bid me abandon this body for a paradise of ideas?

5.

I am an old man, though I hate it,
and wish now to immerse myself in raw color
that its childlike state of grace might envelop me.

Drawing on the beach with a stick
I feel a spirit of delight I seldom find in the studio,

but they wince and beg me to stop,
my canny dealers and rich collectors.

They say there is no money in it.

First I destroyed the old masters and then
I destroyed modern painting
and you ask me why?

Because breaking the mold is what I understood,
tearing down temples and monuments,
releasing the Minotaur from his labyrinth.

Why blood? Why the sword? Why poetry?
Why a dab of ochre for a pear,
why blue apples, why ask such questions?

Why do I go forward, am I a fool, do I believe,
like some superstitious Andalusian peasant,
that painting will enable me to stave off death?

Do not mention that word in my presence!

But I will tell you, since you ask, why I paint.
Lean closer, so I may whisper it.

To stave off death.

The Raspberries (1974)

If it's true, as they teach in elementary school,
that ours is a secular republic, not gods but men
do our temples and sacred monuments adorn,
then how to explain the immediacy with which I recall
my baptism into the cult of American identity,
my consecration as a democratic individual,
the very first things I bought at a store by myself—
a cherry Slurpee in a collectible plastic superhero cup
and a pack of baseball cards, hoping to find Bob Gibson.
This was at the 7-Eleven on Porter Street,
and soon the five-and-dime on Wisconsin Avenue
cycled into orbit, musty aisles of G. C. Murphy Co.
where I might spend my allowance on plastic soldiers,
a balsa wood airplane, a rabbit's foot key chain,
trinkets of no intrinsic worth ennobled by commerce,
aglimmer with the fox fire of mercantile significance,
toys of thought that blazed in the imagination
every step walking home. Not to jingle pocket change,
not to carry a crumpled dollar bill was to drift untethered
from the enormous comfort and safety of the system,
like the astronaut who crosses HAL in *2001: A Space Odyssey,*
like a Stone Age tribe wandering into civilization
from some last unmapped Amazonian tributary.
And what does a child crave more than shelter
within the herd, a shared hymnal of commercial jingles
for toothpaste and tuna fish, sitcoms we eyeballed
like a kaleidoscope refracting fragments
of the shambolic wonder-beast, America, I mean,
because even then TV was not only a magic mirror
but a sociological lens, like the revelatory glasses
Roddy Piper wears in *They Live,* x-ray vision

to lay bare the skeletal urgency of material desire.
Years later, when the Nukak emerged from the rain forest,
their arrival was received as a tragic morality tale,
a corruption of innocence, a postlapsarian seduction,
but the tribesmen expressed little sense of loss
to the journalists, anthropologists and government officials
eagerly gathered at their frontier encampment.
Do you miss your old way of life? Laughter. "No!"
What do you like most about the outside world?
"Hats, pants, frying pans, rice, sugar, matches,
soap, potatoes, onions." *But what about the jungle,*
your mother, in which your people lived as one with nature?
"It's hard catching birds and monkeys for food,"
one hunter explained. "And the caimans have sharp teeth."
A young woman, breast-feeding her infant, said:
"When you walk all day in the forest, your feet hurt a lot."
So much for the garden of Eden. So long, utopia.
Let us bid farewell to Creepy Crawlers and childish things,
to Monopoly and Battleship and Clue in the basement—
Colonel Mustard with the Wrench in the Conservatory,
or was it Colonel Klink, or Colonel Kurtz,
or Lieutenant Calley with the M1 beneath the banyan tree?
Was it Charles Manson or Charlie the Tuna,
the Cisco Kid or Ho Chi Minh? Did it matter?
Did we care? Would we ever learn to tell the difference?
The kaleidoscope churns its color-hoard of shards,
the disco ball radiates random asymmetries,
history streams from the darkness like a deliquescent fable,
a blockbuster narrative we live inside, all together,
like a comically dysfunctional prime-time family,
bound by the limitations of the genre and the paradigm
of the marketplace, bound in a social compact,
a civic order, an ethos of shapeless and elusive liberty
shimmering like the aurora borealis on the horizon,

the way the universe, when you are twelve years old,
swims in and out of focus, too large to hold in the mind
but too urgent to let go of, days and nights
spellbound at the wonder of one's own existence,
all the bafflements and appetites of life on earth
encapsulated in a raindrop sliding down a windowpane,
a ragged feather in a puddle of melting ice,
a song by the Raspberries coming over the radio
to echo in my heart forever.

Orson Welles: Television (1975)

And so the end arrives, in stocking feet,
the great American dream of the movie screen
brought low, domesticated, shrunk to fit,
lions into house cats, forests into lawns,
everything pre-chewed, nibbled at by goldfish,

sold off in dribs and thirty-second spots,
like a taxi meter ticking off the price
to corporate shills in Burbank backlots
of each and every sigh, each song and dance,
each overacted line and misframed shot,

each micronarrative of lust and shame
a carney barker's fable of diminishment,
a parable of what we have become,
each ad for Fab or Glad a meta-myth,
a proof, *reductio ad absurdum.*

And so I hocked my final plum, my pearl,
the blue-ribbon heifer of my baritone—
squandered it all—my voice, my wit, my gall,
my gut, my famous name—*(O softly run,
horses of the night!)*—and sold, like Faust, my soul.

John Ashbery (1976)

That such expression could manifest as variously as light
In a garment of consciousness poses the maker
His first and signal task:
The puzzle of surfaces. How not to recognize this
Face in the mirror, this stream of irreconcilable representations
Flown beyond formal posture to assume
Human dimension, blue-bundled baby or fey homunculus
Sporting dubious headgear,
Mannequin in turban or tea-colored bowler
By turns herculean, effluvial, devout and glib.
Thus to begin

Sheering cross-grain the cheap yard

Goods is one
Approach, gabardine snood
In light melon, form following superficial function,
Hooded, neighborly,
An exercise in mimetic evocation. Or

The manufacture of wallpaper, swaths and swatches
Of meringue organza and lovely taffeta ostrich skin
Stretched like a gallery of Monet astigmatisms
In the Louvre, a penny candy attic of Puvis de Chavannes
In the Louvre. We are always in the Louvre,
Even when we are in Madrid
Spooning pomegranate sorbet. Seeds and myth
At the grand masque of solace, after which renunciation
Tosses her nuptial bouquet to the lions,
A gown of raw silk, oceans of the various

Polymer constituencies, seen and worn, the inhabited
And fabricated, artifice bending its elbow joint
To devise a solution beyond the capacity of the present
Tense to model, as the lightbulb's pewter skull
Reflecting the spewn embers of dawn becomes
A figure for memory remembering itself,
Spark of cognition drawn through time's filament
Into flame. We were like that once, burning,
Aglow, transfigured by vistas of clouds and chimneys,
Mossy terra-cotta where the old urn o'erspills
In a pantomime of surreptitious greed and surrender,
Going through and around, curvilinear, not unplanned for,
Not given to compassion. These astonishing balloons
In the sunrise are feelings, sentimental blimps.
What happens to them assumes the capacity to move
Or to destroy us, severity being a species of fulfillment.
So to find our way toward an untarnished modality,
Lush plateaux above the river, tables on the square
Beneath caroling bells, florid stemware,
Odor of bossy lemons.

But the battle of the seraphic robots
Continues throughout the rainy afternoon
Dismantling the haberdasher's machinery

And nothing can survive it. The finite gleams
Like a revolution in which no goose is cooked,
No rhetoric suborned. Prepared for violent change

The Emperor is crowned with a plastic lobster
While venality totes its own baggage to the depot,
A species of checkroom where what we carry creates
Visceral anxiety, the pain of a phantom limb
Bumped against a sequence of abandoned furnishings

Which are also schools of thought,
An ottoman called Ethics, end tables known as
The Moral Sciences, and so on, and so forth.
Even the river in the foothills resembles a rayon nosegay
Stressed to the point of infarction, glorious
Dialect of a lost tribe of Dutch uncles,
Contemptuous of the harbor lights, yawls and ketches,
Lateen-rigged dinghies so like a cartoonish Mesopotamia,
Links in a dismal chain of indigo inks
From which causality has fled like a rabbit from a hat
Or rats from the ruins of Troy, New York.
Real ruins. Cairns of rubble, sublime
Nuts and bolts, spiked corollas of concertina
Wire, shards, odd morsels, remnants
Wrapped in newspaper dotted with obituaries
And cantaloupe rind.

Sayonara, at long last, to all that
Sorry sheen.

Our small war is over.

Those brash materials, diagrams inscribed upon the dome,
Galaxies burning the ice-blue color of ideas,
The realization that they have constellated us, too,
Fashioned us in their glittering image,
To envision which is to know
The grace of the bare-naked lovers
Enacting their passion in the window display
Of the half-demolished department store at midnight.
Like chocolate poured into silver molds
Beauty seeks its level everywhere,
In coins and kisses, rabbits and stars,
Forming and delimiting whatever can be

Imagined, or spoken, or made, here
Amid the tenebrous, wind-funneled snowflakes at dusk,
Here in the metropolis of rhetorical desire.

Voyager I & II (1977)

Now we begin to speak for you.
To greet, entreat, declaim and argue.

The voices we carry are yours, of course,
your melodies and genetic sequences sourced

and etched into our golden cores.
Like spores

from a broken milkweed plant
we float past planet

after planet, their parabolic array likewise
among the elemental designs

we display. Imagine the moment
of contact, in whichever quadrant

of whichever time-lost galaxy,
when they happen upon us and we

rehearse the tale
of how we first set sail

upon these silent interstellar seas,
replay the encoded dreams and histories

which impel a species
to step into the darkness, to leave

the only home it has ever known
in the hope that it is not alone.

Let there be others, in the great night,
we whisper. Let there be light.

Fernand Braudel: *Civilization and Capitalism* (1978)

Money gave a certain unity to the world but it was the unity of injustice.

1.

Smiths and millers are history's heroes,
tillers and herdsmen who keep the hearth burning,
who have forged, over centuries, a painstaking advance
from hut to croft to homestead, hamlet to township to city.
Kings, generals, revolutionary overlords—
how shallow the imprint of their hammers on time's metal.
History is hills and river valleys, gathering waves
far below the fortified citadel. History is stone idols,
folkways, the stubborn insistence of people to live
where and how they have always lived before.
Populations grow in a simple calculus and fall back
as numbers exceed the carrying capacity of the land,
so many bushels of wheat or yams per acre.
Contraction follows expansion as night follows day:
strong children in woven cradles during times of plenty,
plagues to decimate newly urbanized masses,
cultivated fields reverting to wilderness
and the howls of wolves in abandoned orchards.
Ours, through all recorded ages of the past,
has been a planet of peasants,
and the world that came before history
reveals itself at the margins—hunters and gatherers,
boreal nomads, those few who have eluded civilization's aura,
living witness to the poverty and simplicity
that is our deep inheritance, our universal estate
until the explosive growth of modern times.
Capitalism has become a rocket engine propelling

material betterment toward the stratosphere,
Dark Ages to lunar seas in a handful of centuries.
But the most powerful engines require the richest fuel
and Capitalism runs on toil and suffering.
Predicated upon constant expansion of markets,
which is a mechanical impossibility and a historical lie,
Capitalism is a belief system disguised as a scientific enterprise,
an octopus cloaked in banker's ink, not evil, perhaps,
but certainly amoral and blind to misery.
Capitalism reduces us to numbers on a balance sheet
because numbers do not bleed, equations do not cry out.
No math could be more elemental. Make no mistake,
if you allow another to be bought on the exchange
then you have sold yourself into bondage;
if you consent for any life to be so denominated
you stand complicit and will not be spared.

2.

In a tree above the ruined citadel a hawk has built its nest,
and from that perch looks down at the coastline
of olive groves and fishing boats in rocky coves,
farmers no larger than ants laboring to plant their fields.
The evening is perfumed by lavender and wild roses
climbing the old towers, surrounded now by thickets
and tumbled fortifications where certain stones
still bear the mason's mark—history is in those stones
but history is not a wall, or a tower, or a fortress.
History does not belong to the hawk, however vigilant.
History is an inchworm, a herd of goats, two sparrows.
History is a broken urn, a burrow of field mice,
toadstools and blue irises and the smell of loam after rain,
the rough spears of saplings rushing sunward.
History is seeds and soil. History is survival.

The Nation's Capital (1979)

Because I am seventeen I find a summer job as a dishwasher,
and because it is Washington, DC, I work at the cafeteria
in the East Wing of the National Gallery of Art,
sometimes at the second-story café, beneath the titanic Calder mobile,
the wall-sized Miró tapestry, modernist icons in a structure
of vicious granite angles and streaming tiers of glass.
The city's new subway system remains a colorful diagram,
so I take a bus downtown or borrow my father's Volkswagen
and park along Constitution Avenue at a meter I feed all day.
Inside, the bustling kitchen is a world unto itself,
a long-running soap opera starring middle-aged black women
who manhandle dish racks from scalding-hot ovens,
laughing over the clatter of silverware and stacked mugs.
Mine is the only white face ghosting amidst the steam.
Upstairs, the kitchen is too small for scrubbing, so we
wheel rubber tubs of crockery down the service elevator,
returning with towers of fresh soup bowls and salad plates.
My partner is a lilting, teenaged Jamaican named Tiny
who fills my head with a daylong patter of reggae wisdom
and rumors of the impending death of Bob Marley.
Sometimes we eat beef patties for lunch on D Street,
but most days I spend the hour alone, lost in thought,
reading catalogs in the gift shop or wandering the galleries
until I know every artwork intimately and every painter as a friend.
No, hardly that—they are not a friendly bunch, the Modernists.
Difficult, fractious, stringent, minimalistic or gaudy,
naively intuitive or self-consciously cerebral,
with Picasso lording it over the rest like a Grand Inquisitor.
Even Abstract Expressionism is warmer and fuzzier,
the coy jiggery of Jackson Pollock,
De Kooning's impasto and Rothko's vibrato

and then Lichtenstein's glib nursery rhymes,
Warhol banging a spoon against the bars of his cell
while the history of western art languishes in the classical wing
I visit only to glance at its masterful Van Goghs
before returning to reality with a manila punch card
and a grey rectangular mechanical clock
measuring my life into minuscule denominations
of money and time. Such is the world
I know to expect and want, at any cost, to avoid.
Yet in all those tedious weeks I see nothing on the walls
but visions of the past, hear nothing but echoes
of the retreating footsteps of Japanese tour groups—
for all the hours I stand before Picasso's *Family of Saltimbanques*
I never once hear Rilke's angel incant its elegiac song.
Today, decades later, it is my fondest hope to survive
what remains of my time on this planet
without so much as a whisper from any angel whatsoever,
but how could I have known that then?
I looked, I listened, I studied, I worked,
I felt, I tasted, I wept, I burned.
I rode the bus home, August evenings, past street-corner rhythm men
pounding plastic cans and buckets, and lay awake, after midnight,
beneath a canopy of oak leaves festering with summer heat
and the laments of a million cicadas,
cocooned in my own small, familiar darkness,
listening to Larry King interview some UFO fanatic from Roswell,
some think-tank wonk ranting about the revolutionary mullahs in Iran.
And then a legion of urgent callers joining the conversation
from Topeka and Boise, Huntsville and Rye,
voices from a larger darkness seeking answers to their questions.

BOOK FIVE

Two Poems for Czesław Miłosz (1980)

1. Hills in the Livermore Valley

Swans of grass, sun-swollen apricots, pollen-hoard of almonds
and their bees, their horses grazing orchard rows,
odor of eucalyptus, blown roses, and resinous vineyard dust.
A kestrel hangs unmoving in the updraft
funneled through a saddle-dip
where the big cork oak keels upslope, revealing
the long-term plans of the wind to ripple
just here, at the pass.
Over the ridge the dam-filled lake, golden fields
stitched to the black water's hem,
Umbrian, star-thistled,
verdure of the streams lined with calla lilies
and orange poppies, swifts eating midges below the cattle bridge.

Confronted with beauty in such abundance
the mind balks, like a young lover staggering at the threshold,
a scribe reluctant to acknowledge
the enormity of the account he must commit to paper,

while the body—spilled ink, overripe grapes, cabernet
decanted from an aromatic cask—
pools and fructifies, ages and breathes.

And we, being both, must mediate that conflict,
just as the kestrel, scanning toyon and manzanita for prey,
mediates between the sky and the tapestry of chaparral
unraveling into a wilderness of eastward distance,

born hungry, suspended between realms, looking for a sign.

2. A Castle Surrounded by Chestnut Trees

Turned from the sun, as if in grief,
half earth drinks the pauper's milk of stars.

When morning comes the world that greets the sleepers
is no longer nature's primordial realm
but a planet of old women scattering birdseed,
dark-eyed girls trying to look very grown-up after school,
naïve shrines adorned with pink dahlias,
apple trees crabbed with fruit amid vegetable plots
running down to the train tracks—a pheasant
in the stubble, red and green plumes
like the helmet of a cavalry officer seen in a vision—
the tracks that run to Auschwitz,
the bitter dust of Birkenau spiraling skyward
in billows, a winding sheet, a shroud.

Having made the earth our own, irrevocably,
the contest for its future becomes a human struggle,
moral, ethical, spiritual, rhetorical,
and those undamaged by the brute mechanisms of evil
must live life as a dispensation, a gift,

we, the unbent, the untortured,
must bear witness
to inhumanity wherever it takes root,

in the glyphs and stumble stones,
the keel strakes and roof tiles,
the leaf shudder, the rain-spatter,

among archival fragments, tesserae, lost teeth,

in the candle glow, the tallow reek,
at the last hush, listening
for the shovel-fall of earth upon a coffin lid.

Rain on the Vistula, grey as salt.

Wind in the riverbank rushes and silver willows,
hack of dust at the back of the throat,
burning there, clotting, like poison. The net tightens;

distant mountains bar their passes against me,
the past assembles a cage of falling leaves in air.

I will never escape the twentieth century.

Elegy for Eugenio Montale (1981)

Why should happiness infuse my days through this wick of ink I
burn to write a poem?

Why should grace resemble a drooping lemon tree in its terra-cotta
urn, not a city or a library or a beatitude or a ghost?

How does love endure in a universe of unlegislated molecules, the
stars like silver bearings on which titanic machinery turns?

Yesterday, after gales of rain, the lemon tree glowed as if in rapture,

while all around the garden tiny newborn snails held fast to the tips
of the tallest grasses, waiting for the puddles to recede.

To Héctor Viel Temperley (1982)

I rise straight from the ocean and I am in ecstasy
though I aspire to arrive like a wave

eternally
in progression,

ascent and diminution
as radio transmissions bound for the stars.

My neighbor is a broken man washing his car
again and again in morning sun,

what good is faith without shadow, moonlight

on the dunes,
clouds like ancient murals?

I aspire to rise.
I aspire to rise and fall.

● ● ●

I rise straight from the ocean and I am in ecstasy
digging sand from a dune until my palms bleed,

until the hammer plants
the heel of the hand

with its harsh, romantic kiss.

Because the life of the body bewilders me
no longer, recalling the sweetness
of dates

and rose-apricot jelly,
bitterness
of a radish

scraped against the teeth,

certain the world matters—and yet:

if we had wings would we suffer,
if we had gills?

Children riding imaginary sea horses,
rays and sharks, an ocean of satiation—

my voice does not contain such silk,

listening to the tide's condolence
I hear always the countermelody

at each arrival,
each farewell.

Inexhaustible, the suitcases we will need
to pack away the sorrows yet to come.

•   •   •

I rise straight from the ocean and I am in ecstasy,
proposing faith in a sentence

marching across the page,

simple sentences marching
across the wilderness of the page,

one,
and then—
another.

Beautiful sentences, beautiful sentences!

To which, like cities
in the path of the great Khan's army,
we throw open our gates

lest the obliteration of Urgench
be our portion.

•   •   •

I rise straight from the ocean and I am in ecstasy,
entirely at peace watching a dog cross the drawbridge

like an ambassador from another planet,
sailboats festooned with signal flags, pennants

dripping salt and devotion.

To the poets of the future
        I make but one request on your behalf:

don't just sing it like you mean it.
              Mean it.

      Then sing it.

Georgia O'Keeffe (1983)

Grey is the color of blindness,
but also of sight:
white rocks and black rocks, the moon and her daughter,
equally grey. The door into the dark
is a door into the light,
neither can exist without
its opposite,
women and men, the living and the dead,
we belong to their marriage quarrel,
everything grey
in the cloud-forest of the mind.

Grey of milk in a shadowed pitcher,
grey of goslings, grey of rivets.

Grey being the color of eternity
I commend myself
to its embrace, grey potato skins
slopped for mud-grey hogs, the runted piglet
consumed by its kin,
old snow in the coal-ash arroyo,
almond-husk and violet gravel,
grey as affirmation,
grey as union, the doe at twilight,
the mesa by starlight,
cloud-marked dawn like a brindled flank.

Color of Third Avenue mornings
flush with fresh linen, roman numerals chiseled in basalt,
the Chrysler Building
an awl

to pierce the sheep's caul
through which an airplane descends with bursts of illumination
befitting the immodesty of twentieth-century gods.

Grey as the void
of memory
in which I imagine the feel of a brush
but can't recall its purpose,
cannot envision the cream of jimsonweed, slashed
throat of a dahlia—

what else did god intend me to paint
beyond the flowers
he saw fit to bequeath us,

rocks and flowers, bones
as a last resort.

Color of ghosts, color of clouds and Manhattan,
color of everything
Stieglitz ever photographed, my young body
unrecognizable as the city's erotic stonework—

who is that woman
with hips like the weathered horns of an antelope?

Where has it run to,
in this desert,
the lavish water of her hair?

George Orwell (1984)

When I lie on my side my knees and ankles bang together,
bone touching bone through pliant, implausible layers of skin,
as if foretelling the intimacy they will soon enough regain,
or come to know, clattering with a sound peculiar to bones

tumbled in heaps, in wooden caskets, in shovelfuls of stony earth.
Pure projection, of course, to imagine one's bones imagining
the fleshlessness that awaits them: bones are beams and tent poles,
the body cannot foresee the abyss, as Orwell saw the future,

or had it previewed for him, with peculiar clarity, in Barcelona,
fighting for the Republic during the Spanish Civil War,
when his Trotskyite worker's militia found themselves between
the guns of the Fascists in the trenches and the guns

of their brothers-in-arms, the Communists, who had learned
that it was sometimes more useful to kill friends than enemies,
to strangle a brood-mate, too many hatchlings in the nest.
Useful, though, in what sense? Not to win the war, certainly,

not to bring about the Revolution; useful only in maintaining power.
Power as end and means. So the litany of spies, informers,
disinformation, imprisonment, abduction, torture and murder
compiled during that very minor ideological skirmish in 1936

would be enough to turn anyone bitter and vindictive,
let alone a deeply alienated, misogynistic man like Orwell,
who saw at once that Left or Right mattered not a farthing
to the mint of Totalitarianism coining its bright currency,

stamping the century with black boots and bloodred fists.
Curious that their most powerful weapon would be Orwell's own,
language, propaganda, words uprooted from the soil of meaning,
words torn free of their moorings, boats scuttled in a storm.

Slavery is Freedom, War is Peace, Life is Death. *Et al.*
Of course Winston Smith was a fool not to see it coming,
blinded by utopian lust into complicity in his own downfall,
and Edward Snowden seems less Orwell than Winston Smith.

Of course Big Brother is watching—as he watched in Ur
and Nineveh, peering down from his thatch-shaded ziggurat
to spot rebels, usurpers, messiahs, bandits, rivals of any stripe.
What's changed is the technology and apparatus of power

not the state's desire to suppress, dominate and control.
Ruling elites perch like cattle egrets upon a herd
whose individuality they dissolve into triumphal narratives
of divine intent, or class solidarity, or racial purification.

Orwell, dry-eyed cynic, would never have credited this edition
of 1984, this future not of dystopian scarcity but profusion
to beggar his socialist dreams, the West triumphant,
cracks running everywhere through the spalling pedestals

of the Autocrats—a world in which a McDonald's sign
on the Via Propaganda does not raise a single Roman eyebrow
in ironic commentary—papal cross replaced by Golden Arches
though the orthodoxy remains, the sales pitch, the paperwork.

Still, democracy is a young horse in an old race, let it savor
its garland of roses. Let Stalin's empire perish unmourned.
Let sledges shatter the blocks of tyranny into fragments
from which new walls may be fashioned, stronger walls

for harsher masters. Let the people have their moment,
banners in hand, statues toppling, children held aloft,
their symbols of solidarity already taken up by the marketplace
in ads for Swiss watches and Japanese cars, their slogans

co-opted by the very power they have cast into the shadows
to lick its wounds and seek out better PR consultants.
The twenty-first century will dawn, hungover, reeking of liberation,
and what then? How to keep the Gulags from refilling?

And yet, what else to believe in, even Orwell wondered,
what besides these people and the words they chant—
liberty, justice, equality—whose very utterance, however fleeting,
however contested, denotes a faith in some common future

beyond the boot in the face forever. *Peace, solidarity, freedom.*
Just that. Against fear and oppression, against the tyrants,
against the ideologues, against the darkness, just that.
Words in the mouth of a truth-hungry man.

Orson Welles: The Life (1985)

Somewhere, somehow, I strayed from the righteous path.
I lost my way, like melancholy Dante,
in the *selva oscura* of Hollywood. Too young
I slaked my thirst for glory at the well
of star dust, indolence, and wanton flesh.
Such bodies—Rita, Paola, Eartha, Oja—
their names a trill of verbal ecstasy
to help erase the taste of what I lost,
or gave away, or never shot, or shot
and lost to studio hacks like Harry Cohn,
or bowdlerized, or forged, or dreamed and forgot,
or never could forget—Chicago, Cannes,
traveling through Connaught by mule at sixteen;
Broadway at dawn after opening night;
voodoo, *The Shadow,* Dolores Del Rio;
the snowbound boardinghouse in Colorado
where Charlie Kane's last, tortured glimpse of home
makes Agnes Moorehead's gothic silhouette
a monument to childhood bereavement;
my mother's voice, like a cello, as she died;
my father's wastrel ghost invoked in my own
improvidence, my Falstaffian appetites.
What else does memory resemble but
the uncut rushes of a feature film,
slurry of outtakes, axed lines and overdubs
from which a master narrative emerges
frame by frame, sequence by recut sequence,
as my life's quixotic script has been reshot
to skew from comedy to tragedy,
from tragedy back to cautionary farce.
The skill, my friends, is in the editing.

What to cut, what to print, what to transform
with flash pots and flimflam. *Presto chango!*
All art is conjury, deception, magic.
All the world's an audience, and I'm onstage
alone, directing, playing every part,
all seven ages compassed in my girth,
old man at birth, proud youth, *enfant terrible*
unripening to infantile excess,
bathtubs full of ice cream and chorus girls,
small comforts, small indulgences, small lies
just brash enough to get her into bed.
My yarns were hardly worse than the Bard's tall tales
of Rosebuds fixed in time by poetry.
But movies burn too brightly to survive
the gloom of posterity's hive-dark archive.
They shine a brief moment, outdazzling the stars,
and then burn out, fade down, dissolve, go black.
Film dwarfs the power of atomic bombs.
Destruction is child's play, death is a cinch,
what's hard is to shine a light upon the heart,
to illuminate the souls of men and sear
them into incandescent celluloid,
not graveless bones, irradiated ash.
Boozy, waggish, wolfish and ham-handed,
I was what I was and I am what I am,
student, lover, soldier—a prodigy,
a leading man, a fool afraid of nothing now
but death, the IRS and Lady Macbeth.
What's in a name? Best say: this was a man.
Orotund, ursine, hirsute, stentorian,
obese and obsessed, twice-blessed and thrice-cursed,
doomed but undimmed, the one and only Orson.

The Hudson (1986)

My five-year tour of duty in New York City
fell during that downtrodden era when it was dubbed,
not without ironic affection, New Calcutta,
tail end of a decades-long cycle of civic and social change
that left a dank, uneasy detritus at the turn of the tide.
Homeless men wandered into the local diners
to drink bottles of watery ketchup off the lunch counter
before they could be hustled back out to Amsterdam Avenue.
The 103rd Street subway station resembled Beirut,
shattered tiles cascading from collapsing walls,
stairwells with handrails torn from their stanchions
to rust in puddles of urine, everything so far beyond broken
as to be worthless, scabbed with filth and graffiti,
and the lone transit worker in his bulletproof booth
peeking warily from beneath the brim of his uniform cap
like the citizens staring out through grated windows
as if to ask, *what the hell happened?* Ebb years,
which engendered an inevitable counterflood
towards law and order, primness and conformity,
just as the New Formalists proposed to stem
free verse's laxest practices with their familiar praxis
of meter ruled with metronomic regularity,
tuck-pointing brownstones, renaming neighborhoods,
pushing the street people further into the outer boroughs
as the lucre that primed the pump began to gush anew.
New York is a school that can teach you anything,
three-card monte to leveraged buyouts,
Yiddish opera to extreme martial arts,
but what I learned is that what I was learning
was not a field of inquiry but a way of life, a calling,
devotion to a muse who for all her unforgivable beauty

was merely one daughter of the cloud-begirt kingdom of art.
Those were the last years of my grandmother's life,
and I would sometimes ride the subway to 168th Street
to visit her claustrophobic apartment in Washington Heights,
where my parents had been children when upper Manhattan
was a shtetl of Viennese Jews fleeing the specter of *Anschluss*
and Broadway a boreen for thirsty Irish immigrants,
when the cure for a hot summer evening was to ride
the open-top Fifth Avenue bus from Van Cortlandt Park
to Washington Square with your ringleted sisters
harmonizing hit songs by Perry Como and Doris Day.
At her funeral there was more bitterness than sorrow,
and afterwards we were shanghaied on a nostalgic tour
of "the old neighborhood," blocks of neglected tenements
become a teeming, salsa-toned Dominican barrio,
arguing over which building Ralphie Desoto had lived in,
where the parish boundary for St. Rose of Lima fell,
pausing before the most abject crackhouse to recall
the way a ham sandwich wrapped in wax paper
might be expertly tossed from a fourth-story window
if you forgot your lunch on the way to school.
Where did that world of stickball and Buffalo nickels go?
Where now is Ralphie Desoto, Perry Como, Peewee Reese?
Where are Hart Crane's angelic sailors carousing these days?
Where have the New Formalists vanished to,
Whitman's ferry-bound Bowery Boys, Carl Solomon's ghost?
Where else but the past, a river much like the Hudson,
tidal, dynamic, cliff-bound, estuarine, its source
hidden in pine-covered mountains and its mouth disgorging
dioxins and milk crates and sea bass and lost souls
relentlessly into the cold salt flux of the Atlantic.

Andy Warhol: Waterfall of Dollar Signs (1987)

$$$$$$$$$$$$$$$$$$$$$$$$$$$$$$$$$
$$$$$$$$$$$$$$$$$$$$$$$$$$$
$$$$$$$$$$$$$$$$$$$$$$$
$$$$$$$$$$$$$$$$$$$$$$$$$$
$$$$$$$$$$$$$$$$$$$$$$$$$$$
$$$$$$$$$$$$$$$$$$$$$$$$$$
$$$$$$$$$$$$$$$$$$$$$$$$
$$$$$$$$$$$$$$$$$$$$$$$$$
$$$$$$$$$$$$$$$$$$$$$$$$
$$$$$$$$$$$$$$$$$$$$$$$$$
$$$$$$$$$$$$$$$$$$$$$
$$$$$$$$$$$$$$$$$$$$
$$$$$$$$$$$$$$$$$$$
$$$$$$$$$$$$$$$$$$
$$$$$$$$$$$$$$$$$$
$$$$$$$$$$$$$$$$$$
$$$$$$$$$$$$$$$$$$$$$
$$$$$$$$$$$$$$$$$$$$$$$$$
$$$$$$$$$$$$$$$$$$$$$$$$$$$$
$$$$$$$$$$$$$$$$$$$$$$$$$$$$$$
$$$$$$$$$$$$$$$$$$$$$$$$$$$$$$$$
$$$$$$$$$$$$$$$$$$$$$$$$$$$$$$$$$$$$

Joseph Brodsky in Venice (1988)

La Serenissima, in morning light, is beautiful.
But you already knew that.
Palette of honeyed ochre and ship's bell bronze,
water precisely the color of the hand-ground pigment
with which the water of Venice has been painted for centuries,
angled slats of aquamarine chopped by wakes to agate,
matte black backlit with raw opal
and anodized aluminum, rope-work of wisteria, wands
of oleander emerging from hidden gardens. At noon,
near the boatyard of the last gondola maker, a violin echoes
from deep inside an empty cistern.
Lo and behold. *Ecco.*
A swirl of wind-blown ashes from yet another cigarette
and for a moment you see December snow
in Saint Petersburg, the Lion's Bridge, crystalline halo
crowning Akhmatova's defiant silhouette.

Sunset: bitter orange and almond milk,
sepia retinting the canals with cartographer's ink
as you study the small grey lagoon crabs
patrolling a kingdom of marble slabs
descending into the depths; rising almost imperceptibly,
the tide licks at, kisses, then barely spills
across the top step's foot-worn, weed-velveted lip
in slippery caravans, dust-laden rivulets.

So another day's cargo of terrestrial grit
enriches their scuttled realm,
and they make haste, like drunken pirates in a silent film,
erratically but steadfastly, to claim it.

The Berlin Wall (1989)

Men will come to build the wall,
men will come to tear it down,
    with fists, with horns, with hammers.

Men will come to build the wall,
    men will come to tear it down,
with words, with guns, with banners.

    Men will come to build the wall,
men will come to tear it down,
    with gold, with threats, with lawyers.

Drawn by history's mirror,
    with fists, with horns, with hammers,
mounted on dreams of glory,
    with words, with guns, with banners,
armored in truth and virtue,
    with gold, with threats, with lawyers,

men will come to build the wall,
    men will come to tear it down,
men will come to build the wall,
    men will come to tear it down.

Hubble Space Telescope: The Galaxies (1990)

Altar of red smoke in darkness, a life, a précis,

ants in their task-selves, bees in their hive-self dreaming of
the universal city, of Atlantis & its burnished vaults, spectral
bereavement of its ocean-dusk, Rome looted of marble, dark matter
& the dark metropolis of stars,

cities of the text in blossom as the orchid tree proffers its wounds to
the darkness, as the poinciana rails casual flame,

vernix scriptorium, vitruvian scroll of clouds & dreams,

honeybee asleep on the spine of a Ptolemaic cosmography, dung
beetle on the skull of an ibis, jawbone of an antelope splintered by
hyenas,

coral—their ruined groves, their blossoming colonization of rib &
ark, canopic jars, fractal runes around Rho Ophiuchi, exfoliant dust
in bas-relief,

hair of a nymph glossed with jewels as water in a vase of hyacinth, in
a vessel of sunflowers,

structure in the Vela supernova remnant—pillars of light within the
smoke of light within the blue atomic halo of light, its foundry, its
wheel, its vineyard, canted & bound,

its dicta, its quanta, its folly, its thrum,

ramparts, manacles, urns, jeroboams, shroud of hoarfrost upheld
in the blast, figuration in henna & sackcloth, the one who polishes
smooth stones, the one who casts stones into the sea,

centerward, corebound, yolk plume, obsidian spume, spire of the self
keeled & sprung like a bean sprout fledged & garlanded, the crab, the
pestle, egg tooth against a window of luminous agency,

pups, pupae, prayer shawls, the pelican, helicon, homonym,
phoneme, helix & whorl, the hunter & the hunted,

to transpire, to reflect, to mean, to signify, to detect, to obscure, to
reread,

ants in the spilled fermented milk & honey of it, the spoiled grain of it,

boundary marks, blazes, analogs, the owl in the hazelnut tree, the
soul—who calls from the rain of starlight, who answers?

Lee Atwater's Apocalyptic Dream (1991)

Some nights I dream again of how it was when I was whole and
    hale, unhooked from this cancerous IV, untethered, unapologetic,
    when I was King of the 1980s, Iron Lee, World-Shaper Lee,
    whiteboy Lee with a gutbucket Telecaster buckled to my hip,
    because I'm real with the music, the blues belong to me because
    I desire their grace and humanity like a soul or the conscience I
    hear dripping all night but cannot still or tap, like the accents I
    slip into without noticing, talking jive with the brothers at the
    gas station, my beautiful soul brothers.

Even then I know the people will betray me, the President will
    not attend my funeral, as a master shies from the stench of the
    faithful dog lying dead at his feet.

I know because it is my providence to have gazed into the
    secret heart of the Republic and seen the lies and the truths
    intermingled there, my genius to have understood that lies are a
    kind of truth if they get you what you want.

That's how the dream begins, with the wanting and the getting,
    the victory of stolen kisses in Times Square, already the miracle
    appliances whispering chromed proposals to the roost-ready
    gals and home-coming guys newly enlisted for the Great War
    of Material Consumption, boom-boom children now sprung
    and running loose across fulsome lawns and the finned cars
    evolving like prehistoric sharks backward up the ladder, Elvis
    emerging, the hillbilly hepcat, the GI, the rocker, the lounge act,
    the gold-suited Protestant apotheosis of the dream, there it was,
    pneumatic and buffered and fluted with rock and roll,

the world I would inherit, acquire, study, shape, a new world made
literal in the atom-spray of democracy, the political fact of it
amid the anticlimax of Cold War, which too would end in the
uncertainty of victory, which way to turn, the disillusionment
of hegemony, the anxiety of influence, sowing the soil of the
conquered with Egg McMuffins and KFC, Elvis in the house of
suede with his pills and vomit, sorrowing Elvis, in the end, no
rhythm, only blues.

His death was a fraud, of course, a myth, a special op, top clearance,
eyes only, though the clues were obvious, the charade of the
misspelled tomb as empty as Christ's—suffice it to say he slipped
away, he was enabled to slip away, to escape the drugs and the
boys and the underage girls—CIA, NSA, the details remain
obscure, the agency unimportant.

He lived in a cabin in Montana for a decade, he lived in Nevada, a
hermit in a hut of scrapwood amid the ancient bristlecones on
desert peaks, exchanging secrets with Basque shepherds and
Navajo shamans, absorbing their sere wisdom, wizened now,
near-immortal himself, leathered and glorious and tried in the
stony proving grounds like some Old Testament prophet returned
to us, at that moment, for divine and exquisite purpose.

And so we dressed him in a power tie and put him on the stump
and the numbers were insane, the polls unanimous, he was
universally electable, any state in the union, red and white and
blue, two uneventful years in the Senate and he was ripe for the
top, bigger than Kennedy, Reagan, Lazarus.

Sometimes at the rallies we worried the arena might collapse with
the sheer immanent joy of his believers, a kind of love I have
dreamed all my life of finding, dreamed of creating and refining
to suit my purpose, and I made no mistakes, took no prisoners, he

smiled and nodded his way to the White House and then he was beyond me.

Beyond the grasp of the agencies and cabals and interest groups and councils of power, beyond even the money that made slaves of us all.

He was pure and inviolable, emancipated, an embodiment of freedom and justice and of our lives and times and what we stood for, the chosen son resurrected and unleashed with power to rule the globe, to guide us or free us or save us—or what?

To push the button. To rain black fire from the sky. To command the waiting squadrons to rise from the plains of Nebraska, the Polaris submarines and hardened silos disgorging their missiles across the pole toward the vast Asiatic interior, vapor trail and mushroom cloud our emblem, and more, still more, ever more, not just north and east but west and south, not just the Chinese and the Russians but the French and the Pakistanis and the Brazilians and the Saudis, Turks and Czechs, Fijians, Khmer, Masai, friend and enemy alike consigned to the flames, engulfed in the finale of tracer lines across computer monitors,

and it was real, it was our destiny, chosen and inevitable, and I was not weeping or gnashing my teeth there, in the black bunker, in the darkness beneath Cheyenne Mountain, I was mad with delight, tears like slot cars racing down my cheeks, not wishing it but nonetheless expecting it and believing in it, joyful and complete when Elvis begins to sing, in his white robes and long beard, in the cavern of Strategic Air Command, not kitschy, not sad or happy or good or bad but simple and just and true,

mine eyes have seen the glory, as the world explodes in the fire of our righteousness, *he has trampled out the vineyards*, and I'm with him now, rising into a funnel of white light, rising from the pale and damaged body, giddy with the simple changes and progressions, humping out those blues chords like reverential moonbeams bounced off or ingested, rising from the hospital bed with the smile of a child, playing my guitar, free at last.

Digital Clocks (1992)

Nothing is ticking, the clocks are cheap electronic displays
flashing disarticulated red numerals in the darkness.
The Worldwide Web is an egg-slick hatchling, a wobbly-legged colt;
hyperlink is not part of the jargon, *spam* is still canned meat.
Reality television is not yet a buzzword, the joys and sorrows
of the Kardashians remain entirely their own.
Everything is digital but the future will be virtual, the future
will be live-streamed, crowd-sourced, fully interactive.
Bill Clinton becomes president. The Cold War peters out.
The European Union is founded, to polite applause.
Rigoberta Menchú wins the Nobel Peace Prize,
the AIDS quilt is unveiled, McDonald's opens in Beijing.
A Polish astronomer discovers the first extrasolar planets
orbiting the pulsar PSR B1257+12, in Virgo.
The borough of Centralia, Pennsylvania, is condemned
and seized by eminent domain; fires beneath the town will burn,
it is estimated, for another two hundred and fifty years.
The century is long in the tooth, the century is closing up shop,
bringing down the curtain, heading for the exits—
Francis Bacon dies, John Cage and Lawrence Welk die.
Freddie Mercury has decamped, Miles Davis has laid down his horn.
Bruno Bettelheim, Jiang Qing, Martha Graham, Dr. Seuss,
Frank Capra, Ava Gardner and Curtis LeMay are gone.
On a beautiful spring day in Chicago, Sam McGrath is born
and history halts in its tracks—no, history remains blind
to the astonishing arrival of this red-haired infant
with the deeply wrinkled aspect of a wise and ancient ant,
but my own life, so profoundly engaged with the culture,
decouples, in that instant, from its onrushing locomotive.
Time alters. Or I do. We—I—let go of the guide rope,
drop the century's ticker-tape lifeline and drift

into a still pool beyond the pull of historical circumstance.
Exhaustion and exultation—what else happened in 1992?
What were the hit songs, the movies? It's all recoverable,
the data is in the cloud, we have entered the Information Age,
but can you turn back a clock that lacks the metaphor of hands?
What else has been lost with the watchmaker's tools
if not the idea of time as continuum, time as a coiled spring?
Earth orbits the sun but what are hours? Do minutes exist
if we do not hear them tick? A century is a measuring stick,
a heuristic, but where is the glory in *A Love Supreme*
compared with an instant of bird-trilled infant babble?
Against a scraped knee what matters the tragedy of Verdun?
Century of infant teeth & artificial hearts, century
of triumphalism & colostrum. And what else, what else
happened that year we wove a swallow's nest
of baby blankets and teething rings around ourselves?
One Sunday we took Sam to visit his great-grandmother,
Jane, in a room smelling of medicine and sugar cookies,
where, with Sam in her lap, she recalled with vivid
immediacy an event from her own childhood:
she was raised in towns across the north woods of Wisconsin,
her father a foreman following the lumberjacks from mill to mill,
and one night the forest caught fire, the mill town engulfed,
Jane's family racing to escape in a horse-drawn wagon,
swaddled in wet rugs against a storm of sparks and embers.
It was as visceral to her as if it had happened yesterday,
the smell of the dank wool, pine trees bursting into flame—
you could see her descend within herself to that place,
that moment, and draw it forth like water from a well.
You could feel history crowding the room with its shadows,
history embodied in the child of a horse-drawn past
and the child of a technologically unimaginable future
together in a small apartment in a midwestern suburb,
together in the only place we ever inhabit—the present tense,

the human instant. I can still feel it, right now. It's 2016
but I'm there with Jane and the world she summoned—
it's 1903, it's 1992, I'm immersed in it, like lava,
alive in the pulse of it, the gyre and genuflection of it.
What is memory but the instantiation of time within us?
What is history but a chorus of ghosts?
What is the past but that great burning, that forest of ashes,
the sound of horses running through the darkness?

Roberto Bolaño (1993)

> This is my last communiqué from the planet of the monsters.
> —ROBERTO BOLAÑO, *DISTANT STAR*

Walking out in the afternoon he startles at the sight
of a tortoise in the lawn and feels, instantly,
a bottomless chasm of fear opening beneath his feet.
After a moment the tortoise notices him, startles
in its own ancient and methodical manner,
and ambles behind one scraggly leaf of a fern,
craning its neck, thinking itself well hidden.
Soon, calmer, it continues its journey,
shuffling through fallen leaves like an old vagrant,
spare some change, spare some change, creeping at last
behind a red canoe that has lain unused for a decade.
Unsettled, he returns to the desk in his apartment
but cannot say whether the face in the window
is his, exactly. Or nearly. Or not at all.
What claim, then, can any image make upon him?
The smell of fresh-cut grass like the taste
of green beans eaten raw, or nearly;
cherry stems, six or seven on a cocktail napkin,
a lovely bar girl with crossed eyes
as if watching both the past and future at once.
He cannot say for certain that any word,
however intimately held, belongs to him,
so that when, in some remote mountain range
with names derived from the Arabs or Aztecs,
he hears a sudden thunder, a scimitar clash,
he finds that avalanche of phonemes as disturbing
in its nominal actuality as storm clouds.
In this way he is in dialogue with elemental beings.

He reads everything, even bits of paper
he finds blowing down the street—sometimes
he discovers they contain poems he has written
long before and surrendered to the wind.
He finds his own species fascinating and repulsive:
everything human beyond the self—
every cultural construct, every social institution—
reeks of corruption, compromise, delusion.
Utopia, were it to be conceived, would arrive
in this world stillborn, strangled with its own umbilicus.
He imagines it is possible to live one's life contentedly,
like a reptile in the sunshine, like a blade of grass,
but he wouldn't know anything about that, would he?
Fear and trembling at the sight of a tortoise,
fear and trembling. Still, having lived his life
in service to an illusion he feels no regret.
Poetry will save him, he thinks, with no real conviction,
turning a fresh page in his notebook
and writing there, in blue ink, the following lines.

I am trying to focus but the leaves are falling
so fast through the spectacular
gradients of light—sparrow-light, mystery-light, glory-light—
that I cannot
for all these tears and recriminations
tear my eyes away.

Nelson Mandela (1994)

1. 1934: Transkei

Son of my father's third and favorite wife,
they called me Rolihlahla,
a good name for a troublemaker,
and it was not until I began school in Qunu
that I was given an English name by the teacher,
Miss Mdingane, an admirer
of the great admiral of the colonizers.

Sports were my métier, soccer, boxing, stick-fighting,
and while I hated British imperialism
I accepted their rules
and code of honor as my own. Tall and strong,

I was descended of chieftains,
traditional advisors to the king of my people,
but it was not until my initiation ceremony,
when Chief Meligqili spoke to us
as men newly made,
that I understood the burden of that inheritance.

We are slaves in our own country,
tenants on our own soil,
with no strength, no power, no control
over our destiny in the land of our birth.
The flower of the Xhosa nation are dying
so the whites can live a life of unequaled prosperity.

2. 1964: Robben Island

Show me a world that does not belong to kings
or chieftains, then show me the ruler
who will not defend his privilege with violence.

Apartheid is not a unique injustice.

Therefore I do not take personally my persecution
and so subvert every effort to break my will.

Voiceless, I mastered the language of the law.
Underground, I learned to cast no shadow.
Imprisoned, they command me to labor,
hammering rocks in the quarry's harsh sunlight.

Very well: the world has need of gravel
and my enemy, in his arrogance,
has placed the necessary tool in my hand.

3. 1994: Pretoria

Blood is blood. Africa is African.
Black is white is yellow is brown.

If we follow the path of vengeance
our future shall be stained as red as our past.

But forgiveness, too, is our birthright.

If you cannot see your neighbor
as your brother stand on higher ground.

Climb a hill and search these gathered faces
until you recognize in each the smile
of a favorite auntie, a father's careworn eyes.

To see the people thus is to know
that everything must be risked on their behalf.

Freed from bondage we must feed their minds,
nourish their hearts against hatred and division.

The earth is a single homeland,
one resting place for every ancestor.

Beneath the skin we are indistinguishable.

Brown is yellow is white is black.
Africa is African. Blood is blood.

Seamus Heaney (1995)

The tradition, like a poltergeist, inhabits whom it will.
That visitation, those echoings in moss-farmed wells
and dim library shelves, that bounty,
that creek-tinkle of bog music, those uncanny

squarings and crossings of borders and centuries
full of linguistic drift—that voice is poetry.
Nobody really understands how such things begin,
in which Paleolithic cavern lies its proper origin,

but when it takes up residence in cap and coat,
fit to form as lung-warm breath in the trumpet's throat,
its feet as finely turned as shoes upon the farrier's anvil,
and spills forth radiant as river gravel,
then let us toe the master's lines, each and all.
And heaven help his iamb-haunted soul.

Dolly (1996)

Dolly, a female Finn Dorset sheep, was the first mammal to be cloned from an adult somatic cell.

like the mirror   mirror the like

identity is reflection   reflection is identity

spawn the clone   clone the spawn

helix as palindrome   palindrome as helix

Dolly and Martha   Martha and Dolly

aab aab   *baa! baa!*

Jobs v. Gates: The Mind-Body Debate (1997)

Steve Jobs for the Body

    once Henry Ford built cars to carry people
    as computers now convey
    the unstoppable binary flux of information
    in a machine which must remain functional
    and might as well be beautiful

Bill Gates for the Mind

    data is not a garden snail
    it does not need a plastic shell
    machines are nothing
    but mechanical toys for distractible children
    what matters is the system

Jobs for the Body

    we ourselves are machines of bone and meat
    the body is our only home
    systems crash but we endure
    power corrupts the mighty fall and the weak
    shall inherit the market

Gates for the Mind

    the program is mightier than the sword
    as a species we are defined by brainpower

our flaws are etched in the source code
of our DNA and the body
is a poorly engineered commodity

Jobs

the body is erotic and sensual
full of hard drives and swooping curves
the world of appetite echoes in its carnal well
I pity those too irretrievably geeky
to appreciate the body's glory

Gates

consciousness is sexy
because consciousness sells
you have no products and your company is bankrupt
open the Window and smell the roses
Stevie boy

Steve

nice glasses dork

Bill

I am the richest man in the world

Steve

soon we will destroy you

Bill

    's like attacking the ocean
    with water balloons

Steve

    soon we will destroy you
    with multicolored portable music players

Bill

    oh for heaven's sake. . . .

Steve

    attack, attack!
    destroy, destroy!

                (The debate breaks down.)

1998: The Word for Dylan

Searching for the word for Bob Dylan tonight—*ornery, prophetic,*
     magisterial—old muleskin and buckshot Bob, bindle-stiff Bob in
     glad rags and bolo tie,
sorcerer Bob, straw-into-gold Bob, twinned king and harlequin,
     prince and Rumpelstiltskin, half rattlesnake, half Rumi,
boozy Bob, maudlin and woozy Bob, Big-Bill-Broonzy Bob, boogie-
     woogie Bob, zoot suit Bob, shambolic Bob,
aura of the bird of paradise as written by some Old Testament seer,
     Jeremiah stoned in the wings, vale of sorrows in a hollow-body
     guitar,
wrought-iron Bob graven in cold steel, deep-dyed, jailhouse tattooed,
     inked in peacock plumage, and now the Texas swing, jump blues,
transcending all genres, embodying all hues—*reverent, prismatic,*
     elemental—imperious as the color black, off-white, indigo and
     dandelion,
wail and twine of the high and lonely continental slide, cool and
     celebratory Bob with wide lapels and smiles all around,
bardic Bob, Sephardic Bob, seraph-with-a-flaming-sword Bob—
     gravid, telluric, enrapt—stained-glass Bob gigging with ghosts,
glad-handing brass monkeys, line dancing into the land of gardenia
     and honeysuckle perfume, and it helps to be a river,
helps to be a summer night in old Quebec on the banks of the *fleuve*
     Saint-Laurent beneath a sarabande of stars,
helps to believe in the rock of the continent, *l'Amérique profonde,*
     helps to be polyphonic, Francophone, feedback like a dial tone,
helps it is the first concert we have taken our kids to see and Jackson
     so little he falls asleep in his mother's lap
but still an encounter with the continuum, the tradition, root cellar of
     the lexicon, unrefined ore of the demotic,
voice like quarried granite, voice like cigarette burns in the carpet of
     a roadside motel in the Iron Range of Minnesota,

voice like a temple bell tolling, rolling, groove-worn register to which
    it cleaves like a bowling ball to warped lumber,
organ riffs and slide guitar, grace notes, fables of closure—*luminous,*
    cobalt, antediluvian—canonical Bob bearing our burdens,
blood-and-guts Bob, floodwater Bob in the Mississippi Delta washing
    our troubles away, taking us down, bringing it all back home.

Pentatina for Five Artists (1999)

Art is memory.
Art is ego.
Art is money.
Art is fire.
Art is ashes.

Ashes are time's war paint.
Memory is the history of an individual mind.
Fire is a genius of transformation.
Ego is the seed of identity.
Money is pure sex.

Sex is a socially constructed narrative, or just sex.
War paint is to the self as Easter dye to eggs.
Identity is our floodwall against a sea of others.
The mind is a sponge, or a spiderweb, or a web aggregator.
Transformation composes an erasure poem of the past.

The past is a cultural forest, and also a forest fire.
Sex is money, baby, and money is also money.
Web aggregator, entelechial spider-mind of memory!
Egg of dust, o loneliness, o bride of ashes.
Others; othernesses; other as self: the Other is ego.

Ego is the art of Cindy Sherman.
Fire is the art of Cai Guo-Qiang
Ashes are the art of Anselm Kiefer.
Money is the art of Jeff Koons.
Memory is the art of Louise Bourgeois.

Prologue (2000)

Century of wraiths & indeterminacy.

Century of silicon, century of oil & isotopic dust,
century of honey & plutonium, o radiant century,
o eager, anguished, totalitarian century!

Eagle-taloned century, crumb-tongued century,
abandoned empires, Colony Collapse Disorder:
the bees are dying & with them all our metaphors.

Civilizations are born in the dawn of ideas.
Culture endures as habit, folklore, the Lares,
household gods haunting familiar ruins.
Ideas possess histories not as boats create wakes
but as clouds cast numinous shadows upon the earth,
as archetypes possess resonance, seashells volume,
words both origins & ascensions—language
as baker's yeast, as nectar to the hive, as honeycomb,
as organism, a culture nourished & grown,
hence: cultivation: cultivar, rice or wheat or taro,
yeastless cakes cooked hurriedly on flat stones
in the embers as the tribe moves on,
before dawn, in search of—in search of what?
Food, safety, home? The idea of home?
The idea of the idea, pure haven of meaning?

What can it mean, in a century of fire,
to sound that long Odyssean moan—*home*—
widemouthed orison of birth & origin,
cave-mouth of the future, well-mouth of the past?

Century of devastation, century of loss, like all the others.

Chronos raises his hammer, a bronze bell chimes.

When, during the Great Leap Forward,
as millions perished in famines of his making,
Chairman Mao contemplated replacing the name
of every Chinese citizen with a number,
the vast authoritarian machinery of the twentieth century
reached its numbing & inevitable apogee.

And when he shied from that stroke, the mute
apparatus of history ground forward unperturbed.

Dust will consume us, the ruins of our cities
become salt & ash, & still the brave astronauts
who plant a flag in the iron dirt of Mars
will bear the human burden of oxygen & names.